American Business Bankruptcy

For J. and V.
Two crazy ladies

American Business Bankruptcy

A Primer

SECOND EDITION

Stephen J. Lubben

Harvey Washington Wiley Chair in Corporate Governance and Business Ethics, Seton Hall University, School of Law, USA

Cheltenham, UK • Northampton, MA, USA

Published by
Edward Elgar Publishing Limited
The Lypiatts
15 Lansdown Road
Cheltenham
Glos GL50 2JA
UK

Edward Elgar Publishing, Inc.
William Pratt House
9 Dewey Court
Northampton
Massachusetts 01060
USA

A catalogue record for this book
is available from the British Library

Library of Congress Control Number: 2021936647

This book is available electronically in the **Elgar**online
Law subject collection
http://dx.doi.org/10.4337/9781800379206

ISBN 978 1 80037 919 0 (cased)
ISBN 978 1 80037 920 6 (eBook)

Typeset by Columns Design XML Ltd, Reading
Printed and bound by CPI Group (UK) Ltd, Croydon, CR0 4YY

Contents

PART V   TRANSNATIONAL BUSINESS BANKRUPTCY
         UNDER CHAPTER 15

Author biography

Stephen J. Lubben holds an endowed chair in Corporate Governance at Seton Hall University, School of Law, in Newark, New Jersey, and from 2010 to 2017 he was the "In Debt" columnist for the *New York Times'* Dealbook business page. He is the author of a leading *Corporate Finance* legal textbook, the third edition of which was published in 2020, and *The Law of Failure: A Tour Through the Wilds of American Business Insolvency*. He has been widely quoted by courts and the media on American chapter 11 cases, and has been retained as an expert in insolvency cases around the world. He previously practiced law with the New York and Los Angeles offices of Skadden, Arps, Slate, Meagher & Flom LLP, as a member of the corporate restructuring department.

Preface

This is a short introduction to American business bankruptcy, designed for the law student, junior attorney, or even not-so-junior, non-bankruptcy or non-American attorney who wants to understand the law without necessarily becoming an expert in the field. In particular, I have written this book conscious of the fact that the reader's time is not infinite, and thus I have worked hard to include enough to give the reader a sophisticated view of business bankruptcy, without going too far into fine detail.[1]

This book is about business bankruptcy under federal law, not about state debtor-creditor law.[2] As a general matter, state law provides one or more mechanisms for an unsecured creditor to become a secured creditor, and as such to collect its claim from the debtor's property.[3] Thus, a contractual creditor might obtain a judgment against the debtor for breach of the contract, then give that judgment to a legal official (typically a sheriff or marshal), who goes to the debtor's place of business to find things that can be sold to satisfy the judgment. Or the creditor might file the judgment with a governmental office and thus create a lien on the debtor's real estate. That lien entitles the unpaid creditor to be paid when the property is sold, and might even entitle the creditor to conduct a foreclosure sale of the property.

---

[1] For those looking for more detail on a particular point, all of the major American online legal databases have bankruptcy treatises: Lexis (Collier's on Bankruptcy); Westlaw (Norton Bankruptcy Law & Practice), and Bloomberg Law (the Bloomberg Law Bankruptcy Treatise). Some are also available as paper books too.

[2] For an overview of state collection law, see CHARLES JORDAN TABB, THE LAW OF BANKRUPTCY 10–30 (1997).

[3] Debtor and creditor are terms that law students routinely stumble over: remember, the debtor is the one that *owes* the money; the creditor is the one that is *owed* the money. The debtor is in debt. Creditors can include voluntary lenders, like banks or bondholders, or involuntary creditors, like tort victims or governments (who do not get to choose their taxpayers).

State debtor-creditor law favors the diligent, so that the first creditor to get a judgment and enforce it will often recover more than later creditors. In contrast, bankruptcy provides a collective forum for all creditors (and other stakeholders), in which they can assert their claims against the debtor in a single, federal proceeding.[4] For this reason, some view bankruptcy as a deviation from the natural order, as represented by state contract and property law.[5]

The book primarily focuses on two chapters of the United States Bankruptcy Code – chapters 7 (liquidation) and 11 (reorganization).[6] The final Chapter summarizes the Code's chapter 15, which is of special relevance to international businesses. Many will want to refer to the Bankruptcy Code while reading this book: in the footnote, I provide a link to a free copy online.[7]

Chapter 7 is a simple procedure for business liquidation. A trustee is appointed, who gathers all of the debtor's assets, sells them for cash, and distributes the proceeds to creditors. It is mostly used by small businesses, and by larger businesses after they either attempt to reorganize or sell their assets under chapter 11. The chapter's most economically important role may be serving as a baseline for creditor recoveries in chapter 11.

Because management is displaced with a trustee – who often has no connection with the business – chapter 7 is seen as a poor tool

---

[4]   As explained by one well-known (former) bankruptcy professor:

I see bankruptcy as an attempt to reckon with a debtor's multiple defaults and to distribute the consequences among a number of different actors. Bankruptcy encompasses a number of competing—and sometimes conflicting—values in this distribution. As I see it, no one value dominates, so that bankruptcy policy becomes a composite of factors that bear on a better answer to the question, "How shall the losses be distributed?"

Elizabeth Warren, *Bankruptcy Policy*, 54 U. CHI. L. REV. 775, 777 (1987) (footnotes omitted).

[5]   *E.g.*, Dewsnup v. Timm, 502 U.S. 410, 435 (1992) (Scalia, J. dissenting) ("a bankruptcy law has little to do with natural justice ..."). A wealth of academic scholarship is also based on the notion that bankruptcy should largely mirror state law entitlements. This body of scholarship largely rejects the notion that the Bankruptcy Clause of the Constitution gives Congress substantive powers with regard to bankruptcy.

[6]   The Bankruptcy Code appears in title 11 of the United States Code, to be distinguished from chapter 11 of the Bankruptcy Code itself. Thus, a formal cite to part of chapter 7 would appear as 11 U.S.C. § 707, for example. For ease, throughout this book I simply cite to the "Bankruptcy Code."

[7]   https://www.law.cornell.edu/uscode/text/11 accessed 3 April 2019.

for preserving the value of the debtor's assets. But it still might be preferable to state law for winding down a business that has obviously failed. Federal law is more expensive than simply abandoning a corporation under state law, but federal law also is more transparent and might convince creditors that the debtor's shareholders are "doing the right thing."

Chapter 11 is famous as the tool for reorganizing big businesses like Sears, General Motors, Pacific Gas & Electric Co. (twice), Toys "R" Us, Trump Entertainment Resorts (twice), Adelphia Communications, Kodak, Tribune Group, Texaco, and every major American airline (save for Southwest and JetBlue, so far). One storied airline – Trans World Airlines (TWA) – filed chapter 11 three times before giving up the ghost. But chapter 11 is also a powerful tool for selling a distressed business or for liquidating it in an orderly fashion. Lehman Brothers provides a key example of that use of chapter 11, and we might even include GM, Chrysler and TWA's third bankruptcy in this category as well.

One key difference between chapter 7 and 11 is that in chapter 11, no trustee is appointed (at least not initially). Instead, the debtor's management stays in place, with the powers and duties of a trustee.[8] This arrangement is known as the "debtor in possession" or DIP model. It is unique to the United States.[9]

The rationale is that existing management already knows the company and can lead it into and through bankruptcy with the least disruption. In the process, the DIP can preserve the "going concern" value of the company – the extra value, beyond the liquidation value, of the debtor's assets operated as an ongoing, intact enterprise.

Imagine a company called Bogartco, which is a leading manufacturer of trenchcoats and fedoras. Trenchcoats still sell well, but fedoras have gone out of fashion, and the debts from the fedora side of the business threaten to sink the whole company. Filing a chapter 7 case would displace existing management with a court-appointed trustee who would sell the business, either as a whole or in chunks.

---

[8]   Bankruptcy Code § 1101(1).

[9]   The closest parallel is found in the Canadian Companies' Creditors Arrangement Act, R.S.C. 1985, c. C-36, or CCAA ("C-C-double A"), where the debtor stays in possession but a monitor is also appointed to provide oversight.

But Bogartco would likely shut down in the meantime, because management and most employees would be let go upon filing.

In a chapter 11 case, on the other hand, Bogartco's CEO – call him "HB"[10] – would stay around and, as the representative of the debtor in possession, attempt to negotiate a reorganization plan that would have support of the company's creditors, shareholders, and employees. Part of that plan might include replacing HB with another CEO – after all, he presided over the company's descent into bankruptcy – but that change would not happen on the first day of the bankruptcy case. If the creditors would rather LB take over management, they could seek to include her appointment as part of the deal.

I start the book with key features of the Bankruptcy Code that are common to both chapters 7 and 11, before turning to a more specific look at each chapter in turn. In some instances, I had to make a decision about where to place topics: for example, professionals are employed in chapter 7, but they arguably play a bigger role in chapter 11, so the reader will find a chapter on bankruptcy professionals with the chapter 11 materials.

Again, the goal is to make this easy on the reader, both in terms of time and effort. I welcome your feedback on whether I have succeeded, and what I might improve if and when I update the book.

I owe a special thanks to Thomas Green, Bob Lawless and Will Moon for their comments on early drafts of this book. My former Skadden colleague Peter Clapp is owed special and effusive thanks for not only providing extensive substantive comments, but also providing helpful stylistic and organizational comments throughout the manuscript.

My wife, Jennifer Hoyden, was an invaluable resource in planning and developing this project. She is so very important.

New York
Tuesday, December 4, 2018

---

[10]   https://en.wikipedia.org/wiki/2HB accessed 3 April 2019.

Table of cases

Table of legislation

Table of the Bankruptcy Code (Title 11, United States Code), as amended

PART I

Business bankruptcy basics

1. Some historical context

Key concepts:

- The origins of the Bankruptcy Code
- Equity Receiverships
- The Chandler Act
- Chapter 11

Understanding that modern chapter 7 (liquidation) comes from a different heritage than modern chapter 11 (reorganization) can help us understand the very different approaches both take to the basic question of business failure. Because they are now united under a single Bankruptcy Code, these two strands of the law often use common terminology. But their aims and goals are quite different.

The current United States Bankruptcy Code, which includes chapters 7 and 11 among other chapters, was enacted on November 6, 1978, and became applicable to bankruptcy cases commenced on or after October 1, 1979. It has been subject to several amendments since, particularly in 1984, 1994, and 2005.

Bankruptcy cases are presided over by a United States bankruptcy judge, a judicial officer of the local district court. There is a bankruptcy court for each judicial district in the country, and the bankruptcy courts have their own clerks offices and courtrooms. The bankruptcy judges, however, are not appointed by the President. Instead, they are appointed by the judges of the Court of Appeals for the district, for a renewable 14-year term.[1]

---

[1] Because bankruptcy judges are not appointed under Article III, the scope of their jurisdiction has given rise to a host of complex constitutional issues, that are probably better dealt with as part of a broader consideration of the federal court system. *E.g.*, Wellness Int'l Network, Ltd. v. Sharif, 135 S. Ct. 1932, 191 L. Ed. 2d 911 (2015).

HOW DID WE GET HERE?

Article I, Section 8 of the United States Constitution authorizes Congress to enact "uniform Laws on the subject of Bankruptcies."[2] To the Founders, a single, uniform federal bankruptcy process was preferable to the plethora of state insolvency laws that were enacted both before and after the Revolution. The Bankruptcy Clause can be seen as part of a larger package of provisions – which includes the better-known Commerce Clause – designed to create a national economy. In short, it represents a Hamiltonian vision of the United States.

But until the 1890s, Congress used its bankruptcy power only sporadically. In the nineteenth century, bankruptcy laws would be passed and then repealed in rapid succession. During long periods of time, there was no federal bankruptcy law at all.

In the early days of the Republic, business bankruptcy was the only bankruptcy, because bankruptcy was limited to individual merchants.[3] In colonial times, and into the years immediately after the Revolution, the English notion that being a gentleman and engaging in business were mutually exclusive largely prevailed. Likewise, legal restrictions kept women out of many professions. Bankruptcy was thus a tool available to a narrow slice of the population – mostly men, who engaged in a specific form of business – and nobody else.

Until at least the 1830s, most business activity was organized in forms that left the entrepreneur fully liable for the debts of the business. Whether sole proprietor or general partnership, the failure of the business also meant the failure of the individual. Because the law provided no discharge for the individual debtor, business failure could mean that the debtor-merchant would be thrown into debtor's prison.

Eventually American bankruptcy law abandoned the English, "merchant only" approach, expanding its coverage to all kinds of debtors. Thus, other business debtors, who might not fit within the narrow definition of "merchant," could now file for bankruptcy. At

---

[2] For more on the Bankruptcy Clause, see Stephen J. Lubben, *A New Understanding of the Bankruptcy Clause*, 64 CASE W. RES. L. REV. 319 (2013).

[3] *See* Troy A. McKenzie, *Bankruptcy and the Future of Aggregate Litigation: The Past as Prologue?*, 90 WASH. U. L. REV. 829, 848 (2013).

the same time, businesses increasingly took on forms that provided for separation between the business and its founders. But it was not until well after the Civil War that corporations could file for bankruptcy, and then the only bankruptcy relief available for indebted companies was liquidation.

Non-bankruptcy law alternatives developed that would avoid the disruption and loss of value associated with liquidation. This was particularly true in the years before 1870, when a corporate charter was a valuable thing secured from a state legislature No creditor would lightly allow it to lapse in a liquidation or corporate dissolution.

In early days, corporations that found themselves in financial distress would reorganize through the traditional mortgage foreclosure process. In most states, buyers at foreclosure sales could take the corporate charter and start anew, free from old creditors and shareholders.[4] Some of the old investors would be allowed into the ongoing company, typically in exchange for providing new capital. For example, shareholders might be allowed a diluted stake in the new company, if they agreed to pay an assessment. But it was really all up to the buyers – and if they wanted to leave all the old claimants behind, they could.

Foreclosure worked well in the early days, when the businesses were single-state operations. But a foreclosure sale could not cross

---

[4] Some states still have these statutes on the books. For example, under the New Jersey statutes, the majority of purchasers of certain public service companies (like railroads):

> may organize such new corporation by electing a president and board of six directors, to continue in office for one year succeeding such meeting, and annually thereafter, on the same day of the month, a like election for president and six directors shall be held to serve for one year. At such meeting such majority shall adopt a corporate name and corporate seal, determine the amount of the capital stock thereof, and shall have power and authority to make and issue certificates therefor to the persons in interest, to the amount of their respective interests therein, in shares of fifty dollars each.

> Such new corporation may then or any time thereafter, create and issue preferred stock to such an amount, and at such times as they may deem necessary, and from time to time issue bonds at a rate of interest not exceeding six per cent per annum, to any amount not exceeding their capital stocks and secure the same by a mortgage of the property, rights, powers, privileges and franchises of such corporation.

N.J. Stat. Ann. § 48:3-24.

state lines, and once businesses began to grow increasingly complex even when in state, the need for a new mechanism grew. This was particularly the case with regard to railroads, who transformed themselves from local operations into large, multi-state networks during the Gilded Age.

The answer was found in receivers appointed by federal courts. Receiverships have a long history: basically, any court of equity can appoint a receiver to manage property that is the subject of competing claims. When appointed by a federal court, the receiver benefited from broader jurisdiction – extending across the entire district, which might comprise the state – as compared with a state court that frequently exercised jurisdiction only within a single county. Moreover, ancillary receiverships could be commenced in adjoining districts to extend the reach of the receivership wherever the railroad might extend.[5]

The receiver would operate the railroad – sometimes selling debt instruments, known as "receiver certificates," and using the proceeds to fix it up – while the parties negotiated a reorganization plan. Then a foreclosure sale would commence, and the railroad's

---

[5] The process was summarized thusly:

In order to start the reorganization the directors of the road usually persuade some friendly creditor who is a resident of some other state than that in which suit will be started, to file a bill in the Federal court of the district where the railroad was incorporated or where the main office is located. Ancillary receivers are then appointed in all the federal districts where the railroad owns property. Bankers and others interested financially in the reorganization form protective committees to solicit and receive deposits of bonds and stock, and to work with the reorganization managers to effect a plan of reorganization. Bills to foreclose mortgage liens on the properties also are filed. At a sale of these properties the reorganization managers and the protective committees use bonds deposited with the protective committees to buy in the property. Non-assentors to the plan of reorganization must be paid off, in cash usually, together with expenses of the proceeding. The equity court as a matter of policy requires the plan to be submitted to it for approval as a condition to confirming the sale ...

The chief criticisms of these equity proceedings were that they were slow, that the expense has been scandalous, that banker dominated protective committees controlled the proceeding for their own benefit, that after going through the whole proceeding, the financial structure of the railroad in question was often worse off than before.

Charles S. Rhyne, *Work of the Interstate Commerce Commission in Railroad Reorganization Proceedings under Section 77 of the Bankruptcy Act*, 5 GEO. WASH. L. REV. 749, 753-55 (1937) (footnotes omitted).

assets would be sold to a new, if similarly named company. For example, the Reading Railroad might become the Reading Railway, with a new capital structure as outlined in the reorganization plan. Dissenters were left behind with claims against the old company.

Thus, when Congress enacted the 1898 Bankruptcy Act, the first permanent federal bankruptcy law in this country, business "bankruptcy" actually encompassed two strands. Companies might be liquidated under the 1898 Act, but an important culture of corporate reorganization had simultaneously developed as part of federal equity jurisprudence.[6] It was the latter that was utilized in the really large business failures of the day.

Corporate reorganization was federalized – that is, became subject to federal bankruptcy law – in the years of the Great Depression, as the result of a variety of converging forces. First, the Supreme Court was increasingly chipping away at the utility of the receiverships, probably as a result of fears that the process was becoming too controlled by insiders. Receivership courts were also making a lot of law, the law of corporate reorganization, something that did not fit easily with the Court's declaration that there "is no federal general common law."[7]

At the same time, the need for corporate reorganization exploded during the Depression for obvious reasons. Congress first responded by codifying the receivership process. But then New Deal reformers – most notably, William O. Douglas of the new Securities and Exchange Commission – began investigating the role of Wall Street banks and law firms in receiverships. The many cases in which these big players were seen to dominate proceedings unfairly, at the expense of smaller, retail investors, provided one rationale for a wholesale revamp of the corporate reorganization system.

The result was 1938's Chandler Act, a collection of important amendments to the 1898 Bankruptcy Act. Railroads were allowed to keep their old receivership style provisions under section 77, but all other businesses would have to reorganize under one of two new

---

[6] At this time, railroads were never allowed to liquidate, and could not file under the federal law until the enactment of "section 77" during the New Deal.

[7] Erie R. Co. v. Tompkins, 304 U.S. 64, 78 (1938). Congress had the power to legislate on the subject of bankruptcies, under the Bankruptcy Clause, but courts did not.

chapters. Chapter X was intended to cover all public companies, and those cases were subject to the oversight of the Securities and Exchange Commission. Big New York banks and law firms were excluded from the process.

Chapter XI was aimed at smaller companies. Under the chapter, the debtor had control over both its own bankruptcy estate and the plan process. In theory secured creditors and shareholders could not have their rights altered by the plan, but they could consent to a modification of their treatment. From 1952 onward, a Chapter XI plan was also not subject to the requirement that it be "fair and equitable," a term the Supreme Court had interpreted to incorporate the "absolute priority rule" from liquidations.[8] As a result, shareholders could retain stakes in bankrupt companies, even when creditors were not paid in full.[9]

While "although it seems clear that the simplified procedures of Chapter XI were designed for small, privately owned debtors," the chapter was used by many public companies that managed to shoehorn themselves in.[10] Eventually this convoluted system of three business reorganization provisions (one for railroads and two for other corporations), operating in conjunction with the traditional liquidation bankruptcy provisions, would need to be rehabilitated. And with the enactment of the 1978 Bankruptcy Code, it was.

Under the new Code, all business reorganization was placed in the new chapter 11, the details of which we will encounter in subsequent chapters. The SEC's role was greatly reduced in cases involving public debtors, and "big city" professionals were largely allowed back into the bankruptcy courts.[11] Suddenly, large law firms had restructuring departments for the first time since the 1930s, and restructuring became an aspect of corporate finance once again.

---

[8] *Allocation of Corporate Reorganizations Between Chapters X and XI of the Bankruptcy Act*, 69 HARV. L. REV. 352 (1955).

[9] See Chapter 17 of this book for more on the absolute priority rule, and its role in a modern setting.

[10] *Discretion Properly Exercised in Relying on Business Prospects to Allow Chapter XI Arrangement of Large Public Corporate Debtor*, 64 COLUM. L. REV. 155, 157 (1964).

[11] This was furthered by amendments in 2005 which allowed more Wall Street banks to potentially advise debtors or committees in chapter 11 cases.

Chapter 7 remained largely as it had been before 1978: a provision for appointing a trustee who would take charge of and sell the bankrupt firm's assets and distribute the proceeds to creditors. Both chapters 7 and 11 reside within the Bankruptcy Code and use a common language as a result. As this brief sketch has made clear, however, they come from very different traditions. And as we will see, sometimes those differences make the common terminology awkward, or even complicated.

Chapter 7 and chapter 11 are both in the current Bankruptcy Code. They both use the same words – but the words have different meanings in many cases.

SUMMARY

While the Constitution gave Congress the power to enact national bankruptcy laws, Congress only really used that power starting in 1898. Corporate bankruptcy involving liquidations was conducted under that law until it was replaced by the 1978 Bankruptcy Code, the subject of much of this book. But corporate reorganization developed under a receivership process that was only federalized in the 1930s. Later that decade, the Chandler Act made corporate reorganization more transparent, but also more byzantine. The Bankruptcy Code's chapter 11 represents a kind of compromise between the receiverships of old, and the concerns that drove the Chandler Act's reforms.

2. The central core of business bankruptcy – section 109

Key concepts:

- The definition of person
- The definition of corporation
- Eligibility for chapter 7
- Eligibility for chapter 11
- Voluntary and involuntary petitions
- Conversion of cases
- Venue considerations

Before a bankruptcy petition is ever filed with a bankruptcy court, the debtor's or creditor's counsel needs to make sure the debtor can actually be a debtor under the desired chapter of the Bankruptcy Code. Section 109 of the Bankruptcy Code, titled "Who may be debtor," identifies which entities are eligible to file under which chapters of the Code. For business debtors, our focus here, the key chapters in question are chapter 7 and chapter 11.[1]

We cover the details of these chapters later in this book, but for now is sufficient to understand that chapter 7 is about wrapping up an insolvent business, while chapter 11 offers the possibility of reorganizing the business. Chapter 7 can be seen as a conclusion, while chapter 11 is more like a reset.

---

[1]   As shown in pathbreaking research by Elizabeth Warren and Robert Lawless, many more sole proprietors file bankruptcy each year, often using chapter 13, than official government statistics would suggest. Robert M. Lawless & Elizabeth Warren, *The Myth of the Disappearing Business Bankruptcy*, 93 CAL. L. REV. 743, 745 (2005). This book focuses on business entities, so we will not discuss chapter 13. Each year a handful of small farms and fishing operations file under chapter 12. Chapter 12 is a kind of blend of chapters 11 and 13. Its focus is on individual farmers, and extremely small farming or fishing entities that are owned by a single family. Bankruptcy Code § 101(18)(B); *see also* Bankruptcy Code § 101(19A)(B).

WHO IS ELIGIBLE FOR CHAPTER 7

Section 109 first provides that "only a person that resides or has a domicile, a place of business, or property in the United States, or a municipality, may be a debtor under this title."[2] Unpacking this a bit, we see that either a person or a municipality can be a debtor under the Code. A person must meet one additional requirement, in that they have to either reside in the United States or have their domicile, do business, or own property in the United States.

But what about corporations? How do they get into bankruptcy? The answer is in section 101 – the Bankruptcy Code's definitions section. Section 101(41) states that the "term 'person' includes individual, partnership, and corporation, but does not include governmental unit."[3] Thus, as a "person," a corporation is eligible for chapter 7.[4]

What about a limited liability partnership? Is that a corporation – because it has limited liability – or a partnership? It is quite common for defined terms to be used within defined terms in section 101, and this is an example. Within the definition of person quoted above, corporation and governmental unit are also defined terms that we can find in section 101. Individual and partnership, however, are not defined in the Code.

The definition of corporation is stated in terms of five things that are included within the definition, and one thing that is not.[5] Starting with the latter first, the Bankruptcy Code makes clear that a limited partnership is not a corporation. What it is is left unstated in the Code, although we might presume a limited partnership qualifies as a partnership for bankruptcy purposes.

The Bankruptcy Code does not refer specifically to limited liability companies ("LLCs") – that organizational form did not

---

2   Bankruptcy Code § 109(a).
3   Bankruptcy Code § 101(41).
4   As with every statute, it is important to consider how terms are defined in the Bankruptcy Code, and not import too much "common sense" into your reading of the provisions. This can be tricky when you first begin to learn the Bankruptcy Code, because it is not always clear which terms will be defined in section 101 – the home to most definitions – and which terms might be defined elsewhere, or not at all. But until you get really familiar with the Code, it is always safest to check section 101, where an array of defined terms are set forth in alphabetical order.
5   Bankruptcy Code § 101(9).

exist in 1978, when the Code became law. Under section 101(9), the term corporation "includes," among other things, joint-stock companies,[6] partnerships where the partners have no personal liability, business trusts, and, somewhat confusingly, unincorporated companies and associations. That is, nearly every business entity besides a general or limited partnership is a corporation for Bankruptcy Code purposes. Limited liability partnerships and limited liability companies are thus treated as *corporations* under the Code,[7] and since few general partnerships are formed these days, most of business bankruptcy involves "corporations" as broadly defined in the Code.

Note what section 109 does not say: there is no requirement that the entity be formed under American law. Indeed, each year dozens of foreign corporations and other foreign entities file bankruptcy petitions in the United States.[8]

There is also no requirement that the entity be insolvent. This stands in stark contrast to the laws in most other jurisdictions. For example, in Canada, the jurisdiction with business bankruptcy law that is most similar to the United States, the Companies' Creditors Arrangement Act, Canada's equivalent of chapter 11, defines a "debtor company" to include only those companies that are insolvent or have committed "acts of bankruptcy," as defined under § 42(1) of the Bankruptcy and Insolvency Act, which means either being insolvent or engaging what amounts to either a fraudulent transfer or a preference.[9] In many other jurisdictions bankruptcy and insolvency are synonymous.

That does not mean that bankruptcy in the United States is an all-purpose tool, designed to solve every business problem. Courts have the power to dismiss cases not filed in "good faith," even

---

[6] These are rare in modern times, at least in the United States, but were essentially general partnerships with freely transferable shares. Or you might think of them as corporations without limited liability.

[7] Either as partnerships where the partners have no personal liability, since LLCs are unincorporated entities, or more directly, we might consider an LLC an unincorporated company or association.

[8] Oscar Couwenberg & Stephen J. Lubben, *Corporate Bankruptcy Tourists*, 70 BUS. LAW. 719 (2015).

[9] COMPANIES CREDITORS' ARRANGEMENT ACT, R.S.C. 1985, C. C-36 § 2(1); *see also* BANKRUPTCY AND INSOLVENCY ACT, R.S.C. 1985, c. B-3 § 42(1). We cover fraudulent transfers and preferences in Part II of this book.

when the cases otherwise meet the requirements of section 109. What precisely constitutes "bad faith" is by design somewhat vague, and we should be concerned that too broad a definition might impose requirements that Congress never intended. Nevertheless, filing a bankruptcy case simply to get out of a state court trial that is going against you, or a contract that has proved disadvantageous, is probably not going to work.

Assuming we have an eligible entity, acting in good faith, how does it show that it has the requisite connection with the United States to satisfy the requirements of section 109(a)? First, note that the prospective debtor must be "a person that resides *or* has a domicile, a place of business, *or* property in the United States." Any one of these will do.

Of course, a corporation incorporated in one of the 50 states has its domicile in the United States. But a non-US entity, contemplating bankruptcy in the US, must have a place of business or property here – simply doing business in the United States is not enough.[10] But it is easy to satisfy this rule – any property in the United States will do: no matter the value or type. And the property could take many forms: contracts with New York choice of law clauses have been held sufficient.[11] Same for retainers held by the debtor's bankruptcy attorneys – which means this requirement could almost be self-fulfilling: a foreign company hires an American law firm, gives it a retainer, and *presto!* – its contingent rights in that retainer constitute property in the US.[12]

WHO IS NOT ELIGIBLE FOR CHAPTER 7

Let's next look at section 109(b), which provides that a "person may be a debtor under chapter 7 of this title only if such person is *not* ..." one of three things. First, railroads are not allowed into chapter 7. Once again, I bet you think you know what a railroad is, but take a look at section 101(44). There we learn that railroad could mean two different things: either a common carrier that

[10] In re Head, 223 B.R. 648, 651 (Bankr. W.D.N.Y. 1998).
[11] In re Berau Capital Res. Pte Ltd, 540 B.R. 80, 84 (Bankr. S.D.N.Y. 2015).
[12] In re B.C.I. Finances Pty Ltd., 583 B.R. 288, 293 (Bankr. S.D.N.Y. 2018).

actually transports goods or people on tracks, or the company that owns the tracks and leases them to somebody else.

The Code doesn't define "common carrier." According to Black's Law Dictionary, a common carrier is a:

> commercial enterprise that holds itself out to the public as offering to transport freight or passengers for a fee. A common carrier is generally required by law to transport freight or passengers without refusal if the approved fare or charge is paid.[13]

So the definition is probably both broader and narrower than you first thought. While the term "railroad" often inspires thoughts of steam engines and boxcars, the definition covers nearly everything that moves on rails, which might include some street cars, monorails, and other things that might not be commonly understood as "railroads." On the other hand, the use of the term of art "common carrier," means that certain railroads will not be covered. For example, a railroad that moves things around a large manufacturing facility does not offer services to the general public, and thus is not a railroad for bankruptcy purposes. That is, it could file for bankruptcy as a normal company.

Why keep railroads out of chapter 7? In short, until the late years of the twentieth century, railroads were viewed as utilities, that could not be shut down without grave harm to local communities. The reality of this conception began to fade after the Second World War, with the growth of the automobile and interstate highways, but it was still (barely) in place when the present Code was drafted in 1978. Chapter 7 liquidation was not seen as compatible with the special function of railroads.

Our next group of excluded debtors consists of a long, confusing list of entities that we might generally term "financial institutions."[14] Under section 109(b)(2), neither a domestic insurance company, bank, savings bank, cooperative bank, savings and loan association, nor building and loan association can file chapter 7.[15] In large part the rationale must surely be that these entities are all

---

[13] BRYAN A. GARNER, BLACK'S LAW DICTIONARY (10th ed. 2014).
[14] But in a more familiar sense than "financial institution" as defined in Bankruptcy Code § 101(22).
[15] Bankruptcy Code § 109(b)(2).

heavily regulated, and most of those regulatory regimes also include their own insolvency systems.

For example, insured banks are typically taken over the FDIC. The FDIC has the expertise to deal with banks; bankruptcy courts and bankruptcy trustees do not.

Understood that way, we can also then appreciate that the final part of section 109(b) excludes foreign financial institutions operating in the US from bankruptcy for similar reasons.[16]

The last entity in section 109(b)(2) – "an uninsured State member bank, or a corporation organized under section 25A of the Federal Reserve Act, which operates, or operates as, a multilateral clearing organization pursuant to section 409 of the Federal Deposit Insurance Corporation Improvement Act of 1991" – is not exactly prohibited from filing chapter 7. It can do so, but only at the direction of the Federal Reserve.

So a person, often a corporation (in the broad, Code meaning of "corporation"), that has a connection to the United States and is not a railroad or financial institution should have no trouble starting a business chapter 7 case.

ELIGIBILITY FOR CHAPTER 11

We can then look at section 109(d), which tells us who can file a chapter 11 case. One broad category is everyone who can file a chapter 7 case, except for a stockbroker or a commodity broker. Stockbrokers and commodity brokers are somewhat like the financial institutions that are excluded from chapter 7, but in this case, there are special provisions in chapter 7 that address bankruptcy cases involving brokers.[17] Congress wanted their cases to stay under those special provisions, so they are not allowed into chapter 11.[18]

---

[16]   Bankruptcy Code § 109(b)(3).
[17]   Subchapters III and IV of chapter 7. *See* Chapter 10.
[18]   Indeed, although the Bankruptcy Code provides for a stockbroker liquidation proceeding, it is far more likely that a failing brokerage firm will find itself liquidated under the Securities Investor Protection Act.

United States Bankruptcy Court for the:

_____Eastern District of Virginia_____
_____(State)_____

Case number *(if known)*: _____ Chapter __11__

☐ Check if this is an
amended filing

Official Form 201
Voluntary Petition for Non-Individuals Filing for Bankruptcy
04/16

If more space is needed, attach a separate sheet to this form. On the top of any additional pages, write the debtor's name and the case number (if known). For more information, a separate document, *Instructions for Bankruptcy Forms for Non-Individuals*, is available.

1. Debtor's Name	Toys "R" Us, Inc.	
2. All other names debtor used in the last 8 years		
Include any assumed names, trade names, and *doing business as* names		
3. Debtor's federal Employer Identification Number (EIN)	22-3260693	

4. Debtor's address

Principal place of business	Mailing address, if different from principal place of business
One Geoffrey Way	
Number Street	Number Street
	P.O. Box
Wayne, New Jersey 07470	
City State Zip Code	City State Zip Code
	Location of principal assets, if different from principal place of business
Passaic County, New Jersey	
County	Number Street
	City State Zip Code

5. Debtor's website (URL)   https://www.toysrus.com

6. Type of debtor

☒ Corporation (including Limited Liability Company (LLC) and Limited Liability Partnership (LLP))

☐ Partnership (excluding LLP)

☐ Other. Specify: _____

Official Form 201   Voluntary Petition for Non-Individuals Filing for Bankruptcy   page 1

Debtor	Toys "R" Us, Inc.	Case number *(if known)*	
	Name		

7. Describe debtor's business

A. *Check One:*

☐ Health Care Business (as defined in 11 U.S.C. § 101(27A))

☐ Single Asset Real Estate (as defined in 11 U.S.C. § 101(51B))

☐ Railroad (as defined in 11 U.S.C. § 101(44))

☐ Stockbroker (as defined in 11 U.S.C. § 101(53A))

☐ Commodity Broker (as defined in 11 U.S.C. § 101(6))

☐ Clearing Bank (as defined in 11 U.S.C. § 781(3))

☒ None of the above

B. *Check all that apply:*

☐ Tax-exempt entity (as described in 26 U.S.C. § 501)

☐ Investment company, including hedge fund or pooled investment vehicle (as defined in 15 U.S.C. § 80a-3)

☐ Investment advisor (as defined in 15 U.S.C. § 80b-2(a)(11))

C. NAICS (North American Industry Classification System) 4-digit code that best describes debtor. See http://www.uscourts.gov/four-digit-national-association-naics-codes .
4521 (Department Stores)

8. Under which chapter of the Bankruptcy Code is the debtor filing?

Check One:

☐ Chapter 7

☐ Chapter 9

☒ Chapter 11. *Check all that apply:*

☐ Debtor's aggregate noncontingent liquidated debts (excluding debts owed to insiders or affiliates) are less than $2,566,050 (amount subject to adjustment on 4/01/19 and every 3 years after that).

☐ The debtor is a small business debtor as defined in 11 U.S.C. § 101(51D). If the debtor is a small business debtor, attach the most recent balance sheet, statement of operations, cash-flow statement, and federal income tax return, or if all of these documents do not exist, follow the procedure in 11 U.S.C. § 1116(1)(B).

☐ A plan is being filed with this petition.

☐ Acceptances of the plan were solicited prepetition from one or more classes of creditors, in accordance with 11 U.S.C. § 1126(b).

☐ The debtor is required to file periodic reports (for example, 10K and 10Q) with the Securities and Exchange Commission according to § 13 or 15(d) of the Securities Exchange Act of 1934. File the *Attachment to Voluntary Petition for Non-Individuals Filing for Bankruptcy under Chapter 11* (Official Form 201A) with this form.

☐ The debtor is a shell company as defined in the Securities Exchange Act of 1934 Rule 12b-2.

☐ Chapter 12

9. Were prior bankruptcy cases filed by or against the debtor within the last 8 years?

If more than 2 cases, attach a separate list.

☒ No

☐ Yes.   District   _____   When _____ MM/DD/YYYY   Case number _____

      District   _____   When _____ MM/DD/YYYY   Case number _____

10. Are any bankruptcy cases pending or being filed by a business partner or an affiliate of the debtor?

List all cases. If more than 1, attach a separate list.

☐ No

☒ Yes.   Debtor   **See Rider 1**   Relationship   **Affiliate**

      District   **Eastern District of Virginia**   When   **09/18/2017** MM / DD / YYYY

      Case number, if known _____

Official Form 201	Voluntary Petition for Non-Individuals Filing for Bankruptcy	page 2

Debtor ____Toys "R" Us, Inc._____ Case number *(if known)* _____
      _{Name}

11. Why is the case filed in *this* district?

Check all that apply:

☐ Debtor has had its domicile, principal place of business, or principal assets in this district for 180 days immediately preceding the date of this petition or for a longer part of such 180 days than in any other district.

☒ A bankruptcy case concerning debtor's affiliate, general partner, or partnership is pending in this district.

12. Does the debtor own or have possession of any real property or personal property that needs immediate attention?

☒ No

☐ Yes. Answer below for each property that needs immediate attention. Attach additional sheets if needed.

Why does the property need immediate attention? *(Check all that apply.)*

☐ It poses or is alleged to pose a threat of imminent and identifiable hazard to public health or safety.

What is the hazard? _____

☐ It needs to be physically secured or protected from the weather.

☐ It includes perishable goods or assets that could quickly deteriorate or lose value without attention (for example, livestock, seasonal goods, meat, dairy, produce, or securities-related assets or other options).

☐ Other _____

Where is the property?

        Number   Street

        City   State   Zip Code

Is the property insured?

☐ No

☐ Yes. Insurance agency _____

      Contact name _____

      Phone _____

Statistical and administrative information

13. Debtor's estimation of available funds

Check one:

☒ Funds will be available for distribution to unsecured creditors.

☐ After any administrative expenses are paid, no funds will be available for distribution to unsecured creditors.

14. Estimated number of creditors

☐ 1-49
☐ 50-99
☐ 100-199
☐ 200-999

☐ 1,000-5,000
☐ 5,001-10,000
☐ 10,001-25,000

☐ 25,001-50,000
☐ 50,001-100,000
☒ More than 100,000

15. Estimated assets

☐ $0-$50,000
☐ $50,001-$100,000
☐ $100,001-$500,000
☐ $500,001-$1 million

☐ $1,000,001-$10 million
☐ $10,000,001-$50 million
☐ $50,000,001-$100 million
☐ $100,000,001-$500 million

☐ $500,000,001-$1 billion
☒ $1,000,000,001-$10 billion
☐ $10,000,000,001-$50 billion
☐ More than $50 billion

Official Form 201   Voluntary Petition for Non-Individuals Filing for Bankruptcy   page 3

| Debtor | Toys "R" Us, Inc. | | Case number *(if known)* | |
| | Name | | | |

16. Estimated liabilities

☐ $0-$50,000 ☐ $1,000,001-$10 million ☐ $500,000,001-$1 billion
☐ $50,001-$100,000 ☐ $10,000,001-$50 million ☒ $1,000,000,001-$10 billion
☐ $100,001-$500,000 ☐ $50,000,001-$100 million ☐ $10,000,000,001-$50 billion
☐ $500,001-$1 million ☐ $100,000,001-$500 million ☐ More than $50 billion

Request for Relief, Declaration, and Signatures

WARNING -- Bankruptcy fraud is a serious crime. Making a false statement in connection with a bankruptcy case can result in fines up to $500,000 or imprisonment for up to 20 years, or both. 18 U.S.C. §§ 152, 1341, 1519, and 3571.

17. Declaration and signature of authorized representative of debtor

The debtor requests relief in accordance with the chapter of title 11, United States Code, specified in this petition.

I have been authorized to file this petition on behalf of the debtor.

I have examined the information in this petition and have a reasonable belief that the information is true and correct.

I declare under penalty of perjury that the foregoing is true and correct.

Executed on ___09/18/2017___
MM/ DD / YYYY

✗ /s/ N. Cornell Boggs, III   N. Cornell Boggs, III
Signature of authorized representative of debtor   Printed name

Title __Authorized Signatory__

18. Signature of attorney

✗ /s/ Michael A. Condyles   Date __09/18/2017__
Signature of attorney for debtor   MM/ DD/YYYY

Michael A. Condyles
Printed name

Kutak Rock LLP
Firm name

901 East Byrd Street, Suite 1000
Number   Street

Richmond   VA   23219-4071
City   State   ZIP Code

804-343-5227   michael.condyles@kutakrock.com
Contact phone   Email address

27807   VA
Bar number   State

Figure 2.1

Who else can get into chapter 11? Railroads, who have their own special subchapter within chapter 11.[19] And also those strange multilateral clearing organizations we saw before, but now they can get into chapter 11 without consulting the Federal Reserve.

So for the average corporation that is neither railroad nor financial institution, there will be a basic choice between chapter 7 and chapter 11. Obviously the content of those two chapters – which we explore in upcoming chapters – drives much of the decision. But there is also a size effect at work here too: larger businesses, even when liquidating, rarely file a chapter 7 case at the outset. Instead, they almost always file chapter 11 no matter what.[20]

HOW TO FILE

Assuming a debtor qualifies under chapters 7 or 11, how does a bankruptcy case get underway? A bankruptcy petition gets the ball rolling. I have reproduced an example of one – Figure 2.1 above.

This is a voluntary chapter 11 petition. Filing a petition under section 301(a) is the only mechanism for commencing a voluntary case under chapters 7, 9, 11, 12, or 13 of the Code, and voluntary cases make up the vast bulk of all bankruptcy cases. The petition must be accompanied by the filing fee.[21]

Under section 301(b), the "commencement of a voluntary case under a chapter of this title constitutes an order for relief under such chapter." That is, without actual action by the court, the Code treats the filing of a voluntary petition as if the court had entered an order commencing proceedings.[22]

Because the filing of a voluntary petition constitutes an order for relief, the date of filing marks the point in time from which several

---

[19]   Subchapter IV of chapter 11.
[20]   Largely because of questions of control, as discussed starting in Chapter 11.
[21]   Bankruptcy Rule § 1006(a). Throughout this book, the "Federal Rules of Bankruptcy Procedure" are cited as "Bankruptcy Rule ___". A copy of the rules can be found at https://www.law.cornell.edu/rules/frbp. As of late 2018, the filing fee for chapter 7 is $335; for chapter 11, $1,717. The fees increase periodically – current amounts can be found on the website for the Administrative Office of the United States Courts.
[22]   *See* Bankruptcy Code § 102(6) ("In this title … 'order for relief' means entry of an order for relief."). The rule is different in municipal bankruptcy cases. Bankruptcy Code § 921(d).

deadlines and time limits are calculated. And the automatic stay, a key feature of bankruptcy that we will discuss in detail later in the book, is triggered by the order for relief.

If you look at Figure 2.1, you will see that the voluntary petition is signed by two parties. First, bankruptcy counsel has to sign – the business entities that we focus on in this book cannot represent themselves in court, they need an attorney. In addition, the petition needs to be signed by the entity.

Of course, since the entity is inanimate, it will have to sign through an agent. This sometimes raises questions of state agency and business associations law, especially when the issue arises whether a petition was property filed, by a person with authority to sign the petition. To resolve these issues, the corporate debtor will typically attach to the petition a copy of a resolution of its board of directors, authorizing (among other things) the filing. We see an example of that in Figure 2.2.

Neither state nor federal law provides a direct answer to the question of who controls a business entity's authority to file for bankruptcy.[23] For example, who can authorize a Delaware corporation to file a bankruptcy petition? The nearest thing to a definitive answer comes from Justice Douglas, writing long ago in a case under the Bankruptcy Act:

> The District Court in passing on petitions filed by corporations under Chapter X must of course determine whether they are filed by those who have authority so to act. In absence of federal incorporation, that authority finds its source in local law ... But nowhere is there any indication that Congress bestowed on the bankruptcy court jurisdiction to determine that those who in fact do not have the authority to speak for the corporation as a matter of local law are entitled to be given such authority and therefore should be empowered to file a petition on behalf of the corporation.[24]

Not so much a definitive answer as a direction to look at state corporate law, which may be very unclear or underdeveloped on this point.

---

[23]   This is not a new problem. *Power of Directors to Institute Voluntary or Involuntary Bankruptcy Proceedings Without Stockholders' Consent*, 50 HARV. L. REV. 662 (1937).

[24]   Price v. Gurney, 324 U.S. 100, 107 (1945).

TOYS "R" US, INC.

OMNIBUS RESOLUTIONS

SEPTEMBER 18, 2017

Effective as of the date written above, the undersigned members of the board of directors, members of the board of managers, individual managers, sole managers and sole members (collectively, the "Board"), as applicable, of the entity first set forth above (the "Company") **HEREBY CONSENT** to the taking of the following actions and **HEREBY ADOPT** the following resolutions by unanimous written consent (this "Written Consent") pursuant to the Company's bylaws or limited liability company agreement, as applicable, and the applicable laws of the jurisdiction in which the Company is organized:

Chapter 11 Filing

WHEREAS, the Board of the Company has considered presentations by the management and the financial and legal advisors of the Company regarding the liabilities and liquidity situation of the Company, the strategic alternatives available to them and the effect of the foregoing on the Company's business; and

WHEREAS, the Board of the Company has consulted with the management and the financial and legal advisors of the Company and fully considered each of the strategic alternatives available to the Company.

NOW, THEREFORE, BE IT,

RESOLVED, that in the judgment of the Board of the Company, it is desirable and in the best interests of the Company, its creditors and other parties in interest, that the Company shall be, and hereby is, authorized to file or cause to be filed a voluntary petition for relief (the "Chapter 11 Case") under the provisions of chapter 11 of title 11 of the United States Code (the "Bankruptcy Code") in the United States Bankruptcy Court for the Eastern District of Virginia (the "Bankruptcy Court"); and

RESOLVED, that any officers of the Company (collectively, the "Authorized Signatories"), acting alone or with one or more other Authorized Signatories be, and they hereby are, authorized, empowered and directed to execute and file on behalf of the Company all motions, papers, documents, or other filings, and to take any and all action that they deem necessary or proper to obtain such relief, including, without limitation, any action necessary to maintain the ordinary course operation of the Company's business.

Retention of Professionals

RESOLVED, that each of the Authorized Officers be, and hereby is, authorized and directed to employ the law firm of Kirkland & Ellis LLP and Kirkland & Ellis International LLP (together, "Kirkland") as general bankruptcy counsel to represent and assist the Company in carrying out its duties under the Bankruptcy Code, and to take any and all actions to advance the Company's rights and obligations, including filing any pleadings;

1

and in connection therewith, each Authorized Officer, with power of delegation, is hereby authorized and directed to execute appropriate retention agreements, pay appropriate retainers, and to cause to be filed an appropriate application for authority to retain the services of Kirkland.

RESOLVED, that each of the Authorized Officers be, and hereby is, authorized and directed to employ the law firm of Goodmans LLP ("Goodmans") as general bankruptcy counsel to represent and assist the Company in carrying out its duties in connection with possible Canadian insolvency proceedings, and to take any and all actions to advance the Company's rights and obligations, including filing any pleadings; and in connection therewith, each Authorized Officer, with power of delegation, is hereby authorized and directed to execute appropriate retention agreements, pay appropriate retainers, and to cause to be filed an appropriate application for authority to retain the services of Goodmans.

RESOLVED, that each of the Authorized Officers be, and hereby is, authorized and directed to employ the law firm of Munger, Tolles & Olson LLP ("MTO") as general bankruptcy counsel to represent and assist each independent director, manager, or member of the Company in carrying out its duties under the Bankruptcy Code, and to take any and all actions to advance the Company's rights and obligations, including filing any pleadings; and in connection therewith, each Authorized Officer, with power of delegation, is hereby authorized and directed to execute appropriate retention agreements, pay appropriate retainers, and to cause to be filed an appropriate application for authority to retain the services of MTO.

RESOLVED, that each of the Authorized Officers be, and hereby is, authorized and directed to employ the firm Lazard Frères & Co., LLC ("Lazard") as investment banker and financial advisor to, among other things, assist the Company in evaluating its business and prospects, developing a long-term business plan, developing financial data for evaluation by its Board, creditors, or other third parties, in each case, as requested by the Company, evaluating the Company's capital structure, responding to issues related to the Company's financial liquidity, and in any sale, reorganization, business combination, or similar disposition of the Company's assets; and in connection therewith, each Authorized Officer, with power of delegation, is hereby authorized and directed to execute appropriate retention agreements, pay appropriate retainers, and to cause to be filed an appropriate application for authority to retain the services of Lazard.

RESOLVED, that each of the Authorized Officers be, and hereby is, authorized and directed to employ the firm Alvarez & Marsal North America, LLC ("A&M") as restructuring advisor to, among other things, assist the Company in evaluating its business and prospects, developing a long-term business plan, developing financial data for evaluation by its Board, creditors, or other third parties, in each case as requested by the Company, evaluating the Company's capital structure, responding to issues related to the Company's financial liquidity, and in any sale, reorganization, business combination, or similar disposition of the Company's assets; and in connection therewith, each Authorized Officer, with power of delegation, is hereby authorized and directed to execute appropriate retention agreements, pay appropriate retainers, and to cause to be filed an appropriate application for authority to retain the services of A&M.

RESOLVED, that each of the Authorized Officers be, and hereby is, authorized and directed to employ the firm of Prime Clerk LLC ("Prime Clerk") as notice and claims agent and administrative advisor to represent and assist the Company in carrying out its duties under the Bankruptcy Code, and to take any and all actions to advance the Company's rights and obligations; and in connection therewith, each Authorized Officer, with power of delegation, is hereby authorized and directed to execute appropriate retention agreements, pay appropriate retainers, and to cause to be filed appropriate applications for authority to retain the services of Prime Clerk.

RESOLVED, that each of the Authorized Officers be, and hereby is, authorized and directed to employ the firm of Joele Frank, Wilkinson Brimmer Katcher ("Joele Frank") as communications consultant to represent and assist the Company in conducting crisis and restructuring communications; and in connection therewith, each Authorized Officer, with power of delegation, is hereby authorized and directed to execute appropriate retention agreements, pay appropriate retainers, and to cause to be filed appropriate applications for authority to retain the services of Joele Frank.

RESOLVED, that each of the Authorized Officers be, and hereby is, authorized and directed to employ any other professionals to assist the Company in carrying out its duties under the Bankruptcy Code; and in connection therewith, each Authorized Officer, with power of delegation, is hereby authorized and directed to execute appropriate retention agreements, pay appropriate retainers and fees, and to cause to be filed an appropriate application for authority to retain the services of any other professionals as necessary.

RESOLVED, that each of the Authorized Officers be, and hereby is, with power of delegation, authorized, empowered and directed to execute and file all petitions, schedules, motions, lists, applications, pleadings, and other papers and, in connection therewith, to employ and retain all assistance by legal counsel, accountants, financial advisors, and other professionals and to take and perform any and all further acts and deeds that such Authorized Officer deems necessary, proper, or desirable in connection with the Company's Chapter 11 Case, with a view to the successful prosecution of each such case.

General

RESOLVED, that, in addition to the specific authorizations heretofore conferred upon each Authorized Officer, each Authorized Officer (and his designees and delegates) be, and hereby is, authorized and empowered, in the name of and on behalf of the Company, to take or cause to be taken any and all such other and further action, and to execute, acknowledge, deliver and file any and all such agreements, certificates, instruments and other documents and to pay all expenses, including but not limited to filing fees, in each case as in such Authorized Officer's (or his designees' or delegates') judgment, shall be necessary, advisable or desirable in order to fully carry out the intent and accomplish the purposes of the resolutions adopted herein.

RESOLVED, that the Board of the Company has received sufficient notice of the actions and transactions relating to the matters contemplated by the foregoing resolutions, as may be required by the organizational documents of the Company, or hereby waives any right to have received such notice.

RESOLVED, that all acts, actions and transactions relating to the matters contemplated by the foregoing resolutions done in the name of and on behalf of the Company, which acts would have been approved by the foregoing resolutions except that such acts were taken before the adoption of these resolutions, are hereby in all respects approved and ratified as the true acts and deeds of the Company with the same force and effect as if each such act, transaction, agreement or certificate has been specifically authorized in advance by resolution of the Board of the Company.

RESOLVED, that each Authorized Officer (and his designees and delegates) be, and hereby is, authorized and empowered to take all actions, or to not take any action in the name of the Company, with respect to the transactions contemplated by these resolutions hereunder, as such Authorized Officer shall deem necessary or desirable in such Authorized Officer's reasonable business judgment, as may be necessary or convenient to effectuate the purposes of the transactions contemplated herein.

This Consent may be executed in as many counterparts as may be required; all counterparts shall collectively constitute one and the same Consent.

* * * * * * * * * * * * * *

4

Figure 2.2

As a result, courts have applied general principles of agency law.[25] Corporate officers do not have any implicit authority to file; they need express authorization by the board.[26] While a board typically needs shareholder approval to proceed with extraordinary transactions, like selling all assets or dissolving, filing a bankruptcy petition is not considered to require such approval.[27] Rather, a board acting alone can put the company into either a chapter 7 or chapter 11 case.[28]

Once a debtor has commenced the case, it is possible to change chapters. A chapter 7 debtor may convert to another chapter at any time, without court approval, so long as the debtor is eligible for relief under the new chapter.[29] A chapter 11 debtor can convert its case to chapter 7, so long as a bankruptcy trustee has not been appointed in the chapter 11 case.[30] When conversion is sought by someone other than the debtor, court approval is required for conversion.

INVOLUNTARY CASES

Bankruptcy cases can also be started by creditors. Initiation of such cases is somewhat more complex, and involuntary cases are much less common than voluntary ones. An example of an involuntary petition, which (as you can might imagine) involves a slightly different form, appears as Figure 2.3.

---

[25]   In re Nica Holdings, Inc., 810 F.3d 781, 790 (11th Cir. 2015); Hager v. Gibson, 108 F.3d 35, 40 (4th Cir. 1997).

[26]   In re Stavola/Manson Elec. Co., Inc., 94 B.R. 21, 24 (Bankr. D. Conn. 1988).

[27]   The rule used to be that a board could file a bankruptcy petition without shareholder approval only if the board could likewise initiate an assignment for the benefit of creditors without shareholder approval. GARRARD GLENN, THE LAW GOVERNING LIQUIDATION § 41 (1935). It would appear that the Supreme Court cut the connection between assignments and bankruptcy in 1933. Royal Indem. Co. v. Am. Bond & Mortg. Co., 289 U.S. 165, 171 (1933).

[28]   In re Giggles Rest., Inc., 103 B.R. 549, 553 (Bankr. D.N.J. 1989).

[29]   Bankruptcy Code § 706(a).

[30]   Bankruptcy Code § 1112(a).

Case 18-10074 Doc 1 Filed 01/12/18 Page 1 of 5

Fill in this information to identify the case:

United States Bankruptcy Court for the:

_____ District of __Delaware__
(State)

Case number (if known): _____ Chapter __11__

☐ Check if this

Official Form 205

Involuntary Petition Against a Non-Individual

12/15

Use this form to begin a bankruptcy case against a non-individual you allege to be a debtor subject to an involuntary case. If you want to begin a case against an individual, use the *Involuntary Petition Against an Individual* (Official Form 105). Be as complete and accurate as possible. If more space is needed, attach any additional sheets to this form. On the top of any additional pages, write debtor's name and case number (if known).

Part 1: Identify the Chapter of the Bankruptcy Code Under Which Petition Is Filed

1. Chapter of the Bankruptcy Code	Check one: ☐ Chapter 7 ☒ Chapter 11

Part 2: Identify the Debtor

2. Debtor's name	Oak HRC New Castle, LLC
3. Other names you know the debtor has used in the last 8 years Include any assumed names, trade names, or *doing business as names.*	
4. Debtor's federal Employer Identification Number (EIN)	☒ Unknown EIN __ – __ __ __ __ __ __ __

5. Debtor's address

Principal place of business	Mailing address, if different
32 Buena Vista Drive Number Street	 Number Street
	P.O. Box
New Castle DE 19720 City State ZIP Code	 City State ZIP Code
	Location of principal assets, if different from principal place of business
New Castle County	 Number Street
	 City State ZIP Code

Official Form 205   Involuntary Petition Against a Non-Individual   page 1

SL1 1500687

Case 18-10074   Doc 1   Filed 01/12/18   Page 2 of 5

Debtor   Oak HRC New Castle, LLC   Case number (if known)_____
                  Name

6. Debtor's website (URL)   http://newcastle-health.com

7. Type of debtor
- ☒ Corporation (including Limited Liability Company (LLC) and Limited Liability Partnership (LLP))
- ☐ Partnership (excluding LLP)
- ☐ Other type of debtor. Specify: _____

8. Type of debtor's business

Check one:

- ☒ Health Care Business (as defined in 11 U.S.C. § 101(27A))
- ☐ Single Asset Real Estate (as defined in 11 U.S.C. § 101(51B))
- ☐ Railroad (as defined in 11 U.S.C. § 101(44))
- ☐ Stockbroker (as defined in 11 U.S.C. § 101(53A))
- ☐ Commodity Broker (as defined in 11 U.S.C. § 101(6))
- ☐ Clearing Bank (as defined in 11 U.S.C. § 781(3))
- ☐ None of the types of business listed.
- ☐ Unknown type of business.

9. To the best of your knowledge, are any bankruptcy cases pending by or against any partner or affiliate of this debtor?

- ☒ No
- ☐ Yes. Debtor _____   Relationship _____
  District _____ Date filed _____   Case number, if known _____
                                             MM / DD / YYYY

  Debtor _____   Relationship _____
  District _____ Date filed _____   Case number, if known _____
                                             MM / DD / YYYY

Part 3:   Report About the Case

10. Venue

Check one:

- ☒ Over the last 180 days before the filing of this bankruptcy, the debtor had a domicile, principal place of business, or principal assets in this district longer than in any other district.
- ☐ A bankruptcy case concerning debtor's affiliates, general partner, or partnership is pending in this district.

11. Allegations

Each petitioner is eligible to file this petition under 11 U.S.C. § 303(b).

The debtor may be the subject of an involuntary case under 11 U.S.C. § 303(a).

At least one box must be checked:

- ☒ The debtor is generally not paying its debts as they become due, unless they are the subject of a bona fide dispute as to liability or amount.
- ☒ Within 120 days before the filing of this petition, a custodian, other than a trustee, receiver, or an agent appointed or authorized to take charge of less than substantially all of the property of the debtor for the purpose of enforcing a lien against such property, was appointed or took possession.

12. Has there been a transfer of any claim against the debtor by or to any petitioner?

- ☒ No
- ☐ Yes. Attach all documents that evidence the transfer and any statements required under Bankruptcy Rule 1003(a).

Official Form 205   Involuntary Petition Against a Non-Individual   page 2

SL1 1500687

Case 18-10074 Doc 1 Filed 01/12/18 Page 3 of 5

Debtor Oak HRC New Castle, LLC
      Name

Case number (if known) _____

13. Each petitioner's claim	Name of petitioner	Nature of petitioner's claim	Amount of the claim above the value of any lien
	Healthcare Services Group, Inc.	Trade	$ 164,712.80
	McKesson Medical-Surgical Minnesota Supply Inc.	Trade	$ 63,291.25
	Medline Industries, Inc.	Trade	$ 34,524.76
		Total of petitioners' claims	$ 262,528.81

If more space is needed to list petitioners, attach additional sheets. Write the alleged debtor's name and the case number, if known, at the top of each sheet. Following the format of this form, set out the information required in Parts 3 and 4 of the form for each additional petitioning creditor, the petitioner's claim, the petitioner's representative, and the petitioner's attorney. Include the statement under penalty of perjury set out in Part 4 of the form, followed by each additional petitioner's (or representative's) signature, along with the signature of the petitioner's attorney.

Part 4: Request for Relief

WARNING -- Bankruptcy fraud is a serious crime. Making a false statement in connection with a bankruptcy case can result in fines up to $500,000 or imprisonment for up to 20 years, or both. 18 U.S.C. §§ 152, 1341, 1519, and 3571.

Petitioners request that an order for relief be entered against the debtor under the chapter of 11 U.S.C. specified in this petition. If a petitioning creditor is a corporation, attach the corporate ownership statement required by Bankruptcy Rule 1010(b). If any petitioner is a foreign representative appointed in a foreign proceeding, attach a certified copy of the order of the court granting recognition.

I have examined the information in this document and have a reasonable belief that the information is true and correct.

Petitioners or Petitioners' Representative	Attorneys
Name and mailing address of petitioner	
Healthcare Services Group, Inc. Name	Joseph H. Huston, Jr. Printed name
3220 Tillman Drive, Suite 300 Number Street	Stevens & Lee, P.C. Firm name, if any
Bensalem PA 19020 City State ZIP Code	919 North Market Street, Suite 1300 Number Street
Name and mailing address of petitioner's representative, if any	Wilmington DE 19801 City State ZIP Code
Patrick Orr Name	Contact phone (302) 425-3310 Email jhh@stevenslee.com
3220 Tillman Drive, Suite 300 Number Street	Bar number 4035
Bensalem PA 19020 City State ZIP Code	State DE
I declare under penalty of perjury that the foregoing is true and correct.	
Executed on 1 / 11 / 2018 MM / DD / YYYY	X /s/ Joseph H. Huston, Jr. Signature of attorney
X ~~Plu~~ , SVP Signature of petitioner or representative, including representative's title	Date signed 1/12/2018 MM / DD / YYYY

Official Form 205   Involuntary Petition Against a Non-Individual   page 3

SL1 1500687

Debtor ___Onk HRC New Castle, LLC_____   Case number *(if known)*_____
              Name

Name and mailing address of petitioner

Medline Industries, Inc.   Joseph H. Huston, Jr.
Name   Printed name

Three Lakes Drive   Stevens & Lee, P.C.
Number Street   Firm name, if any

Northfield   IL   60093   919 North Market Street, Suite 1300
City   State   ZIP Code   Number Street

Name and mailing address of petitioner's representative, if any   Wilmington   DE   19801
                                                           City   State   ZIP Code

Shane Reed   Contact phone (302) 425-3310 Email jhh@stevenslee.com
Name

Three Lakes Drive   Bar number   4035
Number Street

Northfield   IL   60093   State   DE
City   State   ZIP Code

I declare under penalty of perjury that the foregoing is true and correct.

Executed on   1/11/18   X /s/ Joseph H. Huston, Jr.
              MM / DD / YYYY   Signature of attorney

X _____ *D:clofee AIR Sv*   Date signed   1/12/2018
Signature of petitioner or representative. Including representative's title   MM / DD / YYYY

Name and mailing address of petitioner

McKesson Medical-Surgical Minnesota Supply Inc.   Joseph H. Huston, Jr.
Name   Printed name

One Post Street   Stevens & Lee, P.C.
Number Street   Firm name, if any

San Francisco   CA   94104   919 North Market Street, Suite 1300
City   State   ZIP Code   Number Street

Name and mailing address of petitioner's representative, if any   Wilmington   DE   19801
                                                           City   State   ZIP Code

Melanie Brewer   Contact phone (302) 425-3310 Email jhh@stevenslee.com
Name

4345 Southpoint Boulevard #110   Bar number   4035
Number Street

Jacksonville   FL   32216   State   DE
City   State   ZIP Code

I declare under penalty of perjury that the foregoing is true and correct.

Executed on _____   X _____
              MM / DD / YYYY   Signature of attorney

X _____   Date signed _____
Signature of petitioner or representative. Including representative's title   MM / DD / YYYY

Official Form 205   Involuntary Petition Against a Non-Individual   page 4

SL1 1500687

Case 18-10074   Doc 1   Filed 01/12/18   Page 5 of 5

Debtor   Oak HRC New Castle, LLC
         Name

Case number *(if known)*

Name and mailing address of petitioner

Medline Industries, Inc.
Name

Three Lakes Drive
Number   Street

Northfield   IL   60093
City   State   ZIP Code

Name and mailing address of petitioner's representative, if any

Shane Reed
Name

Three Lakes Drive
Number   Street

Northfield   IL   60093
City   State   ZIP Code

I declare under penalty of perjury that the foregoing is true and correct.

Executed on
                MM / DD / YYYY

X _____
Signature of petitioner or representative, including representative's title

Joseph H. Huston, Jr.
Printed name

Stevens & Lee, P.C.
Firm name, if any

919 North Market Street, Suite 1300
Number   Street

Wilmington   DE   19801
City   State   ZIP Code

Contact phone (302) 425-3310   Email jhh@stevenslee.com

Bar number   4035

State   DE

X _____
Signature of attorney

Date signed
              MM / DD / YYYY

Name and mailing address of petitioner

McKesson Medical-Surgical Minnesota Supply Inc.
Name

One Post Street
Number   Street

San Francisco   CA   94104
City   State   ZIP Code

Name and mailing address of petitioner's representative, if any

Melanie Brewer
Name

4345 Southpoint Boulevard #110
Number   Street

Jacksonville   FL   32216
City   State   ZIP Code

I declare under penalty of perjury that the foregoing is true and correct.

Executed on 01 / 11 / 2018
             MM / DD / YYYY

X *14 ___ Credit Manager*
Signature of petitioner or representative, including representative's title

Joseph H. Huston, Jr.
Printed name

Stevens & Lee, P.C.
Firm name, if any

919 North Market Street, Suite 1300
Number   Street

Wilmington   DE   19801
City   State   ZIP Code

Contact phone (302) 425-3310   Email jhh@stevenslee.com

Bar number   4035

State   DE

X Joseph H. Huston, Jr.
Signature of attorney

Date signed   1/12/2018
              MM / DD / YYYY

Official Form 205   Involuntary Petition Against a Non-Individual   page 4

SL1 1500687

Figure 2.3

Section 303(a) limits involuntary petitions to chapters 7 and 11. In addition, creditors cannot commence involuntary cases against farmers, family farmers, or any non-profit entity (identified as "a corporation that is not a moneyed, business, or commercial corporation"). The inclusion of both farmers and family farmers should grab your attention right away – these are defined terms in section 101, and there is a difference between the two. The main thing to note is that "farmer" could include lots of very large corporate agribusinesses, like those found in central California.[31] We are not just talking Old MacDonald here.

The exclusion of non-profits means that it is impermissible to file bankruptcy petitions against most churches, as well as many hospitals, private schools, and even some retail operations. While the burden to establish ineligibility for involuntary bankruptcy rests with the would-be debtor, the eligibility requirements of section 303(a) can be waived. For example, an alleged farmer who does not raise the issue at the outset of an involuntary case is stuck in bankruptcy, and does not retain an option to exit bankruptcy by raising it later.[32] Farmers and nonprofit institutions find additional protection in section 1112(c), which prevents conversion of their chapter 11 cases to chapter 7 without their consent, since nonconsensual conversion would equate to an involuntary chapter 7.

If you look at Figure 2.3, you will see that the involuntary petition is signed by three different creditors and their attorneys.[33] Four avenues for commencement of an involuntary case are available under section 303(b). If the debtor has 12 or more creditors, then an involuntary petition must be signed by three or more creditors with noncontingent claims that are not subject to a dispute as to liability or amount with an aggregate unsecured amount of at

---

[31] Bankruptcy Code § 101(20) defines a "farmer" as a "person that received more than 80 percent of such person's gross income during the taxable year of such person immediately preceding the taxable year of such person during which the case under this title concerning such person was commenced from a farming operation owned or operated by such person." Remember that "person" includes corporations.

[32] In re McCloy, 296 F.3d 370 (5th Cir. 2002) ("… an individual's status as a farmer does not go to the jurisdiction of the bankruptcy court over an involuntary bankruptcy petition, but instead is an affirmative defense that may be waived.").

[33] *See also* In re Taberna Preferred Funding IV, Ltd., 578 B.R. 244 (Bankr. S.D.N.Y. 2017).

least $16,750.[34] If the debtor has less than 12 creditors, then one will do the trick.[35]

Section 303(b)(3)(A) permits an involuntary filing by fewer than all of the general partners in a partnership. Remember that "partnership" for Code purposes includes only general and limited partnerships – but only general partners in either have the ability to file a case. Essentially this provision allows for less than all partners to commence a case, but then subjects case initiation to the procedural protections of involuntary cases.

Finally, section 303(b)(4) allows a foreign bankruptcy trustee or similar person to take control of the United States assets of the foreign bankruptcy estate by filing a bankruptcy petition. This power is in addition to the other powers the foreign representative might have chapter 15.[36]

Section 303(d) creates the mechanism for contesting an involuntary proceeding, while section 303(f) allows the debtor to continue to operate its business in the ordinary course until the court enters an order for relief, or dismisses the petition.[37] You might suspect that such operations will be more than a wee bit difficult. *"Pay no attention to the bankruptcy petition looming over our heads ..."*

Under section 303(h) the court must grant the petition either if the debtor does not contest it, if the debtor is generally not paying its undisputed debts as they become due, or if within the previous 120 days a receiver or similar figure has been granted control over substantially all of the debtor's property under non-bankruptcy law.

For example, in many states a debtor can undergo a procedure known as an assignment or assignment for the benefit of creditors, where the debtor assigns all of its assets to a third party (cleverly called the assignee), who attempts to pay off the creditors best it can. It is quite similar to a chapter 7 case, as you will see. But some

---

[34]   The dollar figure here is one of many in the Code that are subject to periodic increase under section 104. The next update will occur on April 1, 2022.

[35]   In counting creditors, we ignore insiders and those who received transfers voidable under various Bankruptcy Code sections, including §§ 544, 545, 547, 548, 549, and 724(a).

[36]   Covered in Chapter 22.

[37]   The time between the date of the involuntary filing and the date of the entry of the order for relief is commonly referred to as the "gap" period. Creditors who lend in this period are termed "gap creditors." Allowed gap claims are then afforded a third priority under § 507(a)(3).

creditors might prefer to be in federal court, and thus the commencement of a bankruptcy-like proceeding outside of the Bankruptcy Code is grounds for a bankruptcy petition. This is one way in which the Bankruptcy Code has the potential to override most other insolvency law in the United States.

That being said, involuntary petitions are not substitutions for foreclosures and other basic debt collection actions. Among other things, section 303(i) provides for the possibility of a judgment against petitioning creditors upon dismissal of an involuntary petition. As a result, the best use of involuntary petitions, at least in the business context, often involves situations where leaving existing management in place would result in grave harm to the creditors and their ability to collect on their debts. In a case of any doubt, the maddening possibility of being liable to the debtor likely discourages a filing.[38]

WHERE TO FILE

Finally, whoever is filing the petition needs to consider where to file. As noted in Chapter 1, each district court in the United States has a related bankruptcy court. In many districts, the bankruptcy courts have locations outside the main courthouse. For example, in the Southern District of New York, bankruptcy courts sit not only in Manhattan, but also in White Plains and Poughkeepsie, well up the Hudson River from New York City.

The venue rules for bankruptcy cases are not in the Bankruptcy Code but in title 28. Corporations can file their bankruptcy case in their state of incorporation, where they have their corporate headquarters, or where they have significant assets.[39] For large corporations, these three places might be distinct: for example, many debtors might be able to file in Delaware, even if the only connection with that state is incorporation.

A corporation can also file its case in a district where an affiliate has a bankruptcy case already pending. In 2009, this allowed

---

[38] *See generally* Brad E. Godshall & Peter M. Giluhy, *The Involuntary Bankruptcy Petition: The World's Worst Debt Collection Device?*, 53 Bus. Law. 1315 (1998).

[39] 28 U.S.C. § 1408.

Chevrolet-Saturn of Harlem, Inc. to file a chapter 11 petition in Manhattan, and then a related business – General Motors Corporation – to file a related case in front of the same judge, even though it was incorporated in Delaware and had its corporate headquarters in Detroit.[40]

Many critics have objected to this sort of "forum shopping," and legislators have occasionally introduced bills to change these rules.[41] Others have noted that the concentration of most of the very large chapter 11 cases in two districts (the SDNY and Delaware) ensures that the judges in those jurisdictions have ample experience with the reorganization of very large, complex corporations. If the cases were spread around the country, it would frequently happen that a bankruptcy judge with little business bankruptcy experience would preside over cases of great economic import.

More directly, debtors often choose forums based on precedent that might be particularly favorable given the debtor's financial circumstances. Throughout this book, we note several disagreements among the circuits (or even districts) as to how a particular piece of the Code should be interpreted. When your business's survival depends on interpreting the Code a particular way, forum shopping seems much less optional.

---

[40] It bears noting that bankruptcy courts have rejected the obvious trick of incorporating a new subsidiary right before bankruptcy to allow filing wherever the company pleases. In re Patriot Coal Corp., 482 B.R. 718, 744 (Bankr. S.D.N.Y. 2012) ("Notwithstanding the absence of bad faith on the part of the Debtors in filing these cases in the Southern District of New York in literal compliance with section 1408, this Court cannot allow the Debtors' venue choice to stand, as to do so would elevate form over substance in way that would be an affront to the purpose of the bankruptcy venue statute and the integrity of the bankruptcy system.")

[41] In early 2018, Senators John Cornyn, R-TX, and Elizabeth Warren, D-MA, introduced the *Bankruptcy Venue Reform Act of 2018*. If enacted, it would require debtors file in the district "in which the principal assets or principal place of business" are located. Subsidiaries could file in the venue of their parent company, but not vice versa (as in General Motors). There is no indication that passage is imminent.

SUMMARY

When filing a business's bankruptcy case, it is tempting to start by looking at section 301, which outlines how to file a voluntary petition. But section 301 itself makes clear that the proper place to begin is section 109, which specifies who can be a debtor under which chapters.[42] Once we are in section 109, we quickly see the need for reference to section 101, which defines important terms like entity, person, corporation, and railroad. In many cases, definitions are embedded within definitions.

---

[42]   Bankruptcy Code § 301(a) ("A voluntary case under a chapter of this title is commenced by the filing with the bankruptcy court a petition *under such chapter by an entity that may be a debtor under such chapter.*") (emphasis added).

PART II

Elements common to all business bankruptcies

3. The estate and the automatic stay

Key concepts:

- The structure of the Bankruptcy Code
- The bankruptcy estate
- The automatic stay
- Adequate protection of secured creditors

The Bankruptcy Code is codified in title 11 of the United States Codes.[1] Thus, references within the Code to "this title," or references in other federal statutes to "title 11," refer to the Bankruptcy Code as a whole. The Code is subdivided into chapters: as initially enacted in 1978, the Code only had odd numbered chapters, from chapter 1 to chapter 13. In subsequent years, chapter 12 (family farmers) and chapter 15 (recognition of foreign insolvency proceedings) were added.

Chapters 1, 3, and 5 are the subject of this part of the book. With some exceptions, these chapters apply to all bankruptcy cases.[2] Rules that apply only to chapter 7 or 11 cases appear in Chapters 7 and 11, respectively.[3]

---

[1]   As explained in the Introduction, throughout this book citations to Bankruptcy Code § ___ can thus be found in the statute books as 11 U.S.C. § ___.

[2]   Bankruptcy Code § 103(a) ("Except as provided in section 1161 of this title, chapters 1, 3, and 5 of this title apply in a case under chapter 7, 11, 12, or 13 of this title ..."). Bankruptcy Code section 1161 provides that "Sections 341, 343, 1102(a)(1), 1104, 1105, 1107, 1129(a)(7), and 1129(c) of this title do not apply in a case concerning a railroad." As we have noted, railroads are different. Note that chapter 9 (municipal bankruptcy) is not included within section 103(a). *See* Bankruptcy Code § 103(f) ("Except as provided in section 901 of this title, only chapters 1 and 9 of this title apply in a case under such chapter 9."). Bankruptcy Code § 103(a) also provides that chapter 1 and "sections 307, 362(o), 555 through 557, and 559 through 562 apply in a case under chapter 15".

[3]   Similarly, rules applicable only to chapter 9, 12, 13, and 15 cases appear in those chapters of the Code.

Chapter 1 is entitled "General Provisions", chapter 3 is "Case Administration," and chapter 5 "Creditors, Debtors, and the Estate." It is the last chapter that we first turn to in this part of the book, but note that we have already discussed chapter 1 (sections 101 and 109) and chapter 3 (sections 301 and 303) in the prior Chapters of this book.

THE ESTATE

Section 541(a) provides that the "commencement of a case under section 301, 302, or 303 of this title creates an estate."[4] It then goes on to state that the "estate is comprised of all the following property, wherever located and by whomever held," and then lists nearly every form of property one might think of, including "all legal or equitable interests of the debtor in property as of the commencement of the case."

That is quite broad: any and all property, *wherever* located. "To this end the term 'property' has been construed most generously and an interest is not outside its reach because it is novel or contingent or because enjoyment must be postponed."[5]

That is, Bogartco could store its unsold fedoras in a warehouse on the Moon, and section 541 would include both the hats and the warehouse in the estate. More practically, this means that the debtor's property abroad is part of the estate. The bankruptcy court may have trouble enforcing its orders in Sudan, but those that are subject to jurisdiction in the United States need to think long and hard before attempting to collect a debt outside the bankruptcy process.[6] The Code does not provide the debtor with any greater rights in its property than it had before bankruptcy,[7] but whatever those rights, they come into the estate.

---

[4] Section 302 provides for joint cases by spouses, and is thus not part of our consideration of business bankruptcy.

[5] Segal v. Rochelle, 382 U.S. 375, 379 (1966).

[6] Especially when considered in conjunction with the automatic stay, discussed below.

[7] See, for example, Bankruptcy Code § 541(d), which makes clear that if the debtor holds property as a trustee, it is the legal, and not the equitable title that comes into the estate. This provision could apply to constructive trusts, as well as formal trust relationships.

Section 541(b) then provides a detailed, though not exhaustive, list of excluded property *not* included in the estate. The list has grown in size with each decade since section 541's enactment.[8] Section 541(c) swings back the other way, and prohibits attempts to keep property out of the estate by contract or state statutes. For example, imagine Bogartco has paid for a delivery of hat ribbon each February, for the next five years. A term in the ribbon agreement that provides that the ribbon does not have to be delivered if Bogartco enters bankruptcy would be unenforceable.[9]

Interestingly, section 101 does not define the term "estate" itself. The leading bankruptcy treatise tells us that:

> It is this central aggregation of property that promotes the fundamental purposes of the Bankruptcy Code: the breathing room given to a debtor that attempts to make a fresh start, and the equality of distribution of assets among similarly situated creditors, according to the priorities set forth within the Code. It is from estate property that the debtor's creditors will be paid.[10]

What "central aggregation of property" means is itself vague, and discussions of the estate can sometimes take on the manner of a late-night college dorm philosophy debate. But it is perhaps best to think that, on the petition date, the debtor's stuff is no longer the debtor's – it is part of the *estate*.

This can be seen most clearly in the case of an individual who files under chapter 7. The debtor gives the bankruptcy trustee all of her stuff, and the trustee uses that stuff to pay creditors.[11] Meanwhile, the debtor – her debts discharged – gets a fresh start, free from the financial burdens of the past.[12]

---

[8] Section 541(b) was originally enacted with just one subsection but currently contains ten.

[9] These provisions are often referred to as "*ipso facto*" clauses – apparently because using Latin makes things clearer. Section 541(c)(1)(A) and (B) invalidate different types of *ipso facto* clauses.

[10] 5-541 COLLIER ON BANKRUPTCY ¶ 541.01.

[11] More precisely, most of her stuff, since some of the stuff will be exempt from inclusion in the estate. Consult a book on personal bankruptcy for more on that.

[12] Ideally. *See* Katherine Porter & Deborah Thorne, *The Failure of the Fresh Start*, 92 CORNELL. L. REV. 67, 87 (2006).

It is not quite so clear in the business context, because, as we will see, corporate entities do not get a "fresh start" in a chapter 7 proceeding, and in chapter 11 the company's management is the "trustee" and thus the line between old and new debtor becomes rather fuzzy. But it is still helpful to think of all of the debtor's stuff going into a big box, pending the outcome of the bankruptcy case.

Section 542 allows the trustee to gather all the debtor's property that might be held by others on the petition date. Section 543 provides that receivers, assignees, and similar parties[13] under state law insolvency proceedings have an obligation to deliver estate assets upon the commencement of a federal bankruptcy proceeding. Section 545 defeats state laws that attempt to give creditors special secured status only upon commencement of a bankruptcy case.

If the creditor has acted "inequitably," it may find that its otherwise-valid lien or mortgage is lost or that its unsecured claim in bankruptcy is pushed below (*i.e.*, subordinated) relative to the claims of all the other creditors.[14] And, perhaps most importantly, various avoiding powers in sections 544, 547, and 548 – which we cover in Chapter 6 – return assets to the estate. Essentially, the avoidance powers plug up the leaks that might come from gaming the system, enhancing the overall equality of the process. All these provisions make the estate created by section 541 more robust.

THE AUTOMATIC STAY

How then do we protect the stuff in the box from creditors, who would like to grab it (and may have been about to do so before the bankruptcy filing)? You often read that a company has "filed for protection from creditors." That is a reference to the "automatic stay" imposed by section 362(a). Under that section, the filing of a bankruptcy petition "operates as a stay, applicable to all entities," of most attempts to collect a pre-bankruptcy debt.[15] For example, section 362(a)(1) prohibits:

---

[13]   "Custodians" within the meaning of section 101(11).

[14]   Bankruptcy Code § 510(c), which essentially codified the holding in Pepper v. Litton, 308 U.S. 295 (1939).

[15]   Notice that the stay applies to "all entities," not just creditors, but also people acting on behalf of creditors, like state or local sheriffs or marshals. Entities, recall, are defined in § 101 to include "person, estate, trust, governmental unit."

the commencement or continuation, including the issuance or employment of process, of a judicial, administrative, or other action or proceeding against the debtor that was or could have been commenced before the commencement of the case under this title, or to recover a claim against the debtor that arose before the commencement of the case under this title.

Likewise, section 362(a)(3) stays "any act to obtain possession of property of the estate or of property from the estate or to exercise control over property of the estate," and section 362(a)(4) stays "any act to create, perfect, or enforce any lien against property of the estate."[16]

Essentially, the Code draws a line in time: on the petition date, all of the debtor's assets go into the estate, and all pre-bankruptcy collection efforts cease. If creditors are to be paid, it will be through the bankruptcy process.

The stay in section 362(a) is called the "automatic stay" because it goes into force upon filing the petition, without further action by the court. And unlike an injunction or other similar prohibitions on action, it applies whether or not a party has notice of the bankruptcy filing. That is, even non-bankruptcy attorneys need to understand the automatic stay. Actions taken in violation of the stay are void. And intentional violation of the stay can be grounds for contempt of court.

The stay is central to the idea of bankruptcy being about equality, in contrast to the individuality of non-bankruptcy debtor-creditor law. The stay forces creditors into the collective process we call bankruptcy, because it closes off other avenues of collection.

Section 362(b) lists actions that are exempt from the automatic stay. Some are rather obvious: filing for bankruptcy, does not give a company license to ignore relevant regulatory law.[17] Criminal proceedings are not subject to the stay. Lawsuits commenced by the debtor are not subject to the stay (although a defendant's counterclaim against the debtor is stayed). Other exceptions are more

---

[16] If we read Bankruptcy Code § 362(a) very closely, we see that subsections (1), (2), (6), (7), and (8) apply to debtors directly; (2), (3), and (4) apply to property of the estate; and (5) applies to property of the debtor.

[17] Bankruptcy Code §§ 362(b)(1), (b)(4), (b)(14), (b)(15), (b)(25). Subsection (b)(1), the exclusion for criminal actions, is the most general.

technical, like the provisions which exempt many derivative trans-actions from the automatic stay, and some would say, bankruptcy altogether.[18]

The stay applies only to the debtor, its property, and property of the estate. It doesn't apply to affiliates of the debtor. For example, imagine a holding company that has issued bonds and files a bankruptcy petition. Upon filing, the holding company is protected by the stay, and actions against it – for example, by holders of the bonds – and its property (which includes the shares of its subsidi-aries) are stayed. But unless the subsidiaries file separate petitions, all of them remain outside the bankruptcy system. If any of them have guaranteed the parent company's bonds, creditors can sue them to collect on the guarantees.

The Code gives the bankruptcy court a general equitable power to effectuate its decisions, and that might include staying actions against non-debtors.[19] In some cases, bankruptcy courts have "extended" the stay to protect the debtor's management – for example, in cases where the debtor's creditors file lawsuits against the debtor's management, and the court concludes that, unless stayed, those lawsuits would unduly divert management's attention from the debtor's reorganization efforts.

But there are policy arguments against pushing this too far – if a non-debtor wants bankruptcy protection, shouldn't it file its own bankruptcy case? And the Code provision in question does state that the bankruptcy court's equitable powers should be used "to carry out the provisions of this title." That is something less than a wide-ranging commission to "do equity."

"LIFTING" THE STAY

Under section 362(d), a creditor can ask the bankruptcy court to lift the automatic stay. One of the most common grounds for lifting the stay is declining collateral value. As a general rule, the automatic stay denies a secured creditor the right to repossess collateral that

---

[18]   For more on this, see Stephen J. Lubben, *Subsidizing Liquidity or Subsid-izing Markets? Safe Harbors, Derivatives, and Finance*, 91 AM. BANKR. L.J. 463 (2017).

[19]   Bankruptcy Code § 105(a).

has become property of the estate. But what if that collateral is declining in value during the course of the bankruptcy case? It seems unfair to both delay the creditor's right to foreclosure, while also imposing increasing losses on the creditor.

Consider a simple example, where a creditor has lent $1 million to Bogartco, Inc., secured by the company's plant. The plant is worth $750,000, but each year it declines in value by $50,000 because of wear and tear. The lender was about to foreclose on the plant when Bogartco filed its chapter 11 petition. As a result of the filing, the foreclosure was stayed. If the debtor spends a year negotiating a reorganization plan, only to have the negotiations fail and the case convert to a chapter 7 liquidation, the creditor may not recover any more than the value of its collateral, which will have depreciated to $700,000.

For that reason, the creditor is likely to move for relief from stay early in Bogartco's case. The Code gives Bogartco a choice: either return the collateral, or provide the creditor with "adequate protection" of the value of its collateral, as defined in section 361. In this case, "adequate protection" might require Bogartco to pay the creditor $50,000 in cash per year, or to grant a lien against some other property that is worth at least as much as the decline in value of the plant.

Section 361 provides examples of acceptable forms of adequate protection, leaving open the possibility that the creative debtor (or debtor's attorney) might offer up something else that the court could approve as meeting the requirements of the Code. In the language of the Code, the question is whether the new offer provides the "indubitable equivalent" of the creditor's interest in the collateral. The Code also makes clear that one putative form of protection will not cut it: namely, simply providing the creditor with a priority claim will not do.

SUMMARY

A marked shift in the relationship between debtors and creditors occurs upon the filing of a bankruptcy petition. An estate is created, comprising both the legal and economic interests of the pre-bankruptcy debtor. Creditors lose their individual collection rights against the company, and they are obliged to interact with an estate operating on behalf of all the creditors. An automatic statutory "order," the automatic stay, halting actions against the estate goes into place to protect the new estate.

4. Creditors' claims against the estate

Key concepts:

- The definition of claim
- Administrative expenses
- Allowed claims
- Priority claims
- Allowed secured claims
- Setoff

As noted in Chapter 3, the filing of a bankruptcy petition creates an estate and directs creditors to that estate as their source of recovery. Under the Code, a creditor is an "entity that has a claim against the debtor that arose at the time of or before the order for relief concerning the debtor."[1] Recall that entity is in turn defined as including nearly everyone.[2]

Section 101 also defines "claim" very broadly – it includes almost any right to payment, and any equitable right that could be reduced to a money obligation.[3] Indeed, it appears that Congress intended that the definition sweep as broadly as possible.

The definition of "claim" matters in contexts that might not be anticipated. If a creditor fails to assert its "claim" against the debtor, the debtor's bankruptcy may discharge the claim, with no recovery for the creditor.

In one notable example, in *Ohio v. Kovacs*,[4] the State of Ohio obtained a state court judgment against the debtor for violations of

---

[1] Bankruptcy Code § 101(10)(A).
[2] Precisely, "person, estate, trust, governmental unit, and United States trustee." Person and governmental unit are also defined within section 101.
[3] Bankruptcy Code § 101(5).
[4] 469 U.S. 274, 105 (1985).

environmental laws at a hazardous waste disposal site. The judgment included an injunction to clean up the site. When the debtor failed to comply with the judgment, Ohio appointed a receiver who took possession of the property and began to clean up the site. In Kovacs' bankruptcy case, the Supreme Court concluded that because the only thing Ohio sought from Kovacs was reimbursement for the cleanup, the state court cleanup order was a demand for money damages – a "claim" under the Bankruptcy Code. Because the state had not filed a claim in Kovacs' case, it recovered nothing.

What then does *not* constitute a claim? One common example involves non-competition agreements: bankruptcy courts routinely find that such agreements do not constitute claims, because they are best enforced by injunctions, even if we might wonder if they could not be replaced with a (presumably large) damages judgment.[5]

Another limitation comes from the due process clause of Fifth Amendment, in the Bill of Rights. If a person could not possibly know they have a claim – because they have no relationship with the debtor whatsoever – courts routinely hold their claim may not dealt with in the bankruptcy process, even if it otherwise meets the Code's definition of claim. For example, while the owners of defective car might have a claim against a bankruptcy auto manufacturer for an injury that has yet to occur – because claim is defined to include unliquidated, contingent and unmatured rights – the non-owner, non-family member passenger in the car, who is injured post-petition, would not have a claim in the bankruptcy.[6] Whether this is a good or bad thing, from the passenger/future creditor's perspective, will largely turn on whether the debtor survives the bankruptcy case.[7]

Whether an obligation owed by a debtor becomes a claim – and can thus be discharged – also raises a distributional question among competing creditors. If the debtor is liquidating, I (as creditor) will want as few claims as possible to share in the estate that I am claiming against; but if the debtor is reorganizing, I would rather my claim either to pass through the process untouched – because it

---

[5]   *E.g.*, In re Hurvitz, 554 B.R. 35, 39 (Bankr. D. Mass. 2016).
[6]   Epstein v. Official Comm. of Unsecured Creditors of Estate of Piper Aircraft Corp., 58 F.3d 1573, 1577 (11th Cir. 1995).
[7]   If the debtor liquidates, there will be nobody to pay the future claims.

is not deemed a "claim" – or as many claims as possible to be dispatched, because the reorganization might give me a stake in the future company. That is, where I stand the bankruptcy process depends on what I expect to happen to the debtor.

Claims are to be distinguished from shareholder or equity interests in the debtor. Creditors are entities that have "a claim against the debtor that arose at the time of or before the order for relief concerning the debtor." Remember that a claim is a "right to payment," whereas it is basic corporate law that shareholders have no *rights* to get paid. Payments to shareholders – dividends – are always in the discretion of the board.[8]

Under the Code, "equity security holder" means holder of an equity security of the debtor, and equity security is defined to include not only shares of a corporation's stock, but also limited partnership interests and warrants to obtain shares.[9] As we will develop in further chapters, a shareholder has an *interest* in – but not a *claim* against – the debtor.[10]

ADMINISTRATIVE CLAIMS

It is also necessary to distinguish between pre-petition and post-petition claims. Pre-petition claims – customarily called "general unsecured claims" – are debts that the debtor owed before commencing its bankruptcy case.

In contrast, claims that arise after bankruptcy are deemed part of the cost of administering the bankruptcy process and are entitled to priority payment.

Section 503 defines what counts as an "administrative expense," also commonly referred to as an administrative claim. Administrative claims are largely the costs of running the estate post-petition. They include, in a chapter 7 case, the fees and expenses of the trustee and any professionals retained by the trustee, the cost of resolving claims, liquidating the estate's assets, and distributing the

---

[8] Indeed, the one thing that distinguishes preferred shares from subordinated debt is that the shares can remain unpaid, if the board so decides, so long as junior shareholders receive no dividends. Debt is a fixed claim, with specific payment obligations.

[9] Bankruptcy Code § 101(16).

[10] *See* Bankruptcy Code § 501(a).

proceeds. In a chapter 11 case in which the debtor is an operating entity, in addition to expenses directly related to the chapter 11 process, they include the costs of operating the business – inventory purchases, employee salaries, post-petition tax liabilities, and the like. If, after bankruptcy, the debtor commits a tort, the tort liability may be an administrative expense.[11]

One exception to this general rule – pre-petition claims arise before bankruptcy, administrative claims arise after – is section 503(b)(9), which was added in 2005. That provision provides that goods received by the debtor, in the ordinary course of business and within twenty days of the petition filing, constitute administrative expenses. That is, certain trade creditors who supply the debtor on the eve of bankruptcy are treated as if their claims arose post-bankruptcy, rather than pre-bankruptcy. Note that this provision applies only to goods, and not to services.[12]

Other, more traditional, administrative expenses in section 503(b) include estate operating costs and taxes. Although section 503(b)(1)(A) specifically includes wages, salaries, and the like, the use of the term "including" in the statute means that this provision is not limiting and may include other types of costs and expenses.[13]

Section 507 of the Code, which sets forth various priority unsecured claims, provides that administrative expenses claims shall be paid second.[14] In business bankruptcy cases, this is essentially a first priority, since the only prior category involves "domestic support obligations," something that most corporations do not find themselves owing.

---

[11]   Reading v. Brown, 391 U.S. 471 (1968).

[12]   Neither term is defined in the Code, and many courts instead look to the U.C.C. for help. The Code also does not define the term "receipt"; thus, courts have applied the definition of "receipt" of goods found in Article 2 of the U.C.C.

[13]   Bankruptcy Code § 102(3) ("'includes' and 'including' are not limiting."). That provision, of course, simply represents a truth of English grammar, but it is a point that many lawyers forget – hence the inevitable, "including, but not limited to …"

[14]   Bankruptcy Code § 507(a)(2).

FILING AND ALLOWANCE OF CLAIMS

Pre-bankruptcy claims are the very subject of the bankruptcy process. Sections 501 and 502 of the Bankruptcy Code work together here to establish a process whereby potential claims against and interests in the debtor are first identified and then either allowed or disallowed, as appropriate. A few of these claims then will be entitled to special priorities under section 507.

Section 501 starts with the idea that pre-petition creditors need to file "proofs of claim." The Code does not set a deadline for filing claims. Most chapter 7 cases are "no-asset" cases, in which creditors will receive nothing. Accordingly, the chapter 7 trustee will send a notice requesting that creditors file claims by a specified deadline only if it appears that there will be funds to distributed. In chapter 11 cases, the court will set a deadline – called the "bar date" – on the debtor's motion. The bar date is typically several months after the commencement of the case. There is an official proof-of-claim form for use in either case.[15]

In chapter 11, section 1111(a) provides that claims that are listed on the schedules of assets and liabilities filed by the debtor (or chapter 11 trustee) in the case are "deemed" filed proofs of claims under section 501 of the Code, unless the schedules list the claims as "disputed, contingent, or unliquidated." In short, if the creditor agrees with what the chapter 11 debtor says about their claim, there is no need to file a separate proof of claim.

Once claims are filed, we turn to section 502. There we learn that the claim will be allowed in the case, unless somebody objects to it. In short, once filed – actually, or constructively under section 1111(a) – the burden is off the creditor, at least for a while. Even if the claim is defective in some respect, if nobody objects, the claim is allowed.[16]

Section 502(b) provides that if there is an objection, the bankruptcy court, after notice and a hearing, must determine the amount of the claim, fixed as of the date of the filing of the petition. But "notice and a hearing" is a Bankruptcy Code term of art, defined in section 102 to mean notice and maybe a hearing. Namely, if the

---

[15] http://www.uscourts.gov/forms/bankruptcy-forms/proof-claim-0.
[16] *See* Midland Funding, LLC v. Johnson, 137 S. Ct. 1407, 1412, 197 L. Ed. 2d 790 (2017).

debtor objects to a claim and the creditor fails to respond, the court can enter an order disallowing the claim without an actual hearing.

Under section 502(b), the court must allow the claim, unless it falls within one of nine categories.[17] Most notably, section 502(b)(1) instructs bankruptcy courts to disallow claims that are "unenforceable against the debtor" – for example, if it is barred by the statute of limitations or maybe a gambling debt in jurisdictions that do not enforce such contracts. Mostly applicable nonbankruptcy law will determine a claim's validity and legality.

But in at least two cases, section 502(b) limits claims to an amount that is less than the creditor would be entitled to under state law. For example, section 502(b)(6) caps the claim of a landlord, arising from a breached lease, to the unpaid rent on the date of bankruptcy plus the greater of one year's rent or 15 percent of the remaining rent, with this second 15 percent test further capped at three year's rent.[18] This provision contrasts with state law, where the landlord would likely sue to recover rent for the entire remaining term of the lease, probably offset by the rent received from a new tenant, when the landlord happens to find one. Similarly, section 502(b)(7) limits the claim of a terminated employee, for breach of an employment contract, to one year's compensation.

Thus, if Bogartco has forty years left on a lease for a warehouse in Kansas City that it no longer needs, its lawyer will likely advise

---

[17] In addition to the grounds listed in § 502(b), a claim may be disallowed for reasons set forth in § 502(d) and (e).

[18] The text reflects the interpretation most courts have adopted. Another reading of § 502(b)(6), arguably preferable, is that the 15 percent limitation applies to time, rather than dollars. That is, when § 502(b)(6) refers to "15 percent, not to exceed three years, of the remaining term of such lease," it means 15 percent of the time left on the lease. That interpretation works nicely with the further proviso that the recovery may not exceed three years – both limitations then being in temporal, rather than monetary, terms. For example, if the lease were for a 100-year term, the first part of the phrase would allow a claim for 15 years of rent, but that claim would then be capped at three years of rent by the second part of the phrase. Since three years represents 15 percent of twenty years, under this interpretation of the lease, the second phrase is only of relevance in leases with more than twenty years remaining. For a good discussion of this interpretation of 502(b)(6), see In re Filene's Basement, LLC, No. 11-13511 (KJC), 2015 WL 1806347, at *6 (Bankr. D. Del. Apr. 16, 2015). Finally, we might note that the difference in interpretations only matters when the lease provides for increases in the rent, or the rent is otherwise not constant across the term of the lease. But many commercial leases do provide for automatic increases during the lease term.

that, in bankruptcy, it can get out of the lease with a much smaller liability than state law would provide.[19]

Section 502(b)(2) also provides the statutory basis for the fundamental rule that unsecured claims cease to accrue interest upon a bankruptcy filing. That is, no matter how long the bankruptcy case takes to resolve, the creditor's claim on the petition date is their claim for all purposes under the Code. In essence, a bankruptcy filing accelerates all unsecured claims, but it also freezes them. One reason for this is that it places all unsecured creditors on the same footing with regard to the bankruptcy estate, regardless of whether of what they might have bargained for before bankruptcy.

The court's allowance of a claim determines future participation of the creditor in the bankruptcy case. Only holders of allowed claims may vote on chapter 11 plans under section 1126 or receive distributions on their claims in chapter 7 cases or under confirmed plans in chapter 11.

PRIORITY CLAIMS

We have already noted that section 507 provides administrative claimants with a first priority in business bankruptcy cases. Section 507(a) lists eight more types of claims that are entitled to payment before general unsecured creditors. In addition, 507(b) provides a "super-priority" for creditors who received adequate protection that turned out to be inadequate.[20]

Notably, section 364(c)(1) allows courts to give a priority to post-petition lenders that trumps all other priorities. Call it the "super-duper priority." Section 364 is discussed in detail in Chapter 12 of this book.

SECURED CREDITORS

What about secured creditors? Creditors with a lien, mortgage, or other interest in collateral are potentially treated as having two claims under the Bankruptcy Code. Namely, under section

---

[19]   *See* Chapter 5.
[20]   Recall the discussion of adequate protection in Chapter 3.

506(a)(1), a creditor is treated as having a secured claim in an amount up to the value of the collateral, and an unsecured claim for the remainder.

Under section 506(a)(1) creditors have an "allowed secured claim" only to the extent of the value of their collateral. If you then read section 506(d), you might assume that the creditor's lien is cut down to this collateral value.[21]

The Supreme Court rejected that sensible interpretation in *Dewsnup v. Timm*,[22] over the vigorous dissent of Justices Scalia and Souter. Finding that Congress' intentions with regard to 506(d) were unclear, the Court turned to the practice under the old Bankruptcy Act, where bankruptcy only dealt with the debtor's liability on the claim, and did not touch any liens or security interests. In a personal bankruptcy case before 1978, this meant that the individual debtor's bankruptcy would discharge (that is, cancel) the debtor's personal obligation on the debt, but the creditor could still take the collateral after bankruptcy was over. The Court decided this is still the rule under the current Code, at least in chapter 7.

As we will see, in chapter 11 cases it is quite common for debtors to attempt to strip down secured creditor's liens. But that relies on provisions within chapter 11 to overcome the rule of *Dewsnup v. Timm*.

If the secured creditor is over-secured – that is, their collateral is worth more than their claim – they are entitled to special treatment under the Code. Most notably, they can continue to charge interest and any fees provided for in the loan agreement, at least until the total claim balance hits the collateral value.[23]

As we have already noted, secured creditors are also entitled to demand adequate protection of their collateral value. That right to protection applies whether or not the creditor is over-secured. But the right to charge interest is limited to over-secured creditors.

---

[21]   "To the extent that a lien secures a claim against the debtor that is not an allowed secured claim, such lien is void."

[22]   502 U.S. 410, 417 (1992) ("Were we writing on a clean slate, we might be inclined to agree with petitioner that the words 'allowed secured claim' must take the same meaning in § 506(d) as in § 506(a). But, given the ambiguity in the text, we are not convinced that Congress intended to depart from the pre-Code rule that liens pass through bankruptcy unaffected.").

[23]   At which point, the creditor is no longer over-secured.

Under-secured creditors have no right to interest, either under section 506 or as "adequate protection" for the delay in fore-closing.[24] In this respect, under-secured creditors are just like entirely unsecured creditors.

SETOFF AND RECOUPMENT

Under the Bankruptcy Code, creditors with setoff rights are treated pretty much like secured creditors. Setoff is an equitable right that "allows entities that owe each other money to apply their mutual debts against each other, thereby avoiding 'the absurdity of making A pay B when B owes A.'"[25] Section 553 of the Bankruptcy Code recognizes the right of setoff in bankruptcy cases, but the actual base source of such rights will be non-bankruptcy law. A creditor asserting setoff rights in bankruptcy will thus have to show both that it has such rights under law, and that it satisfies the additional requirements of section 553.[26] Moreover, under section 362(a)(7) of the Code, the actual exercise of a right of setoff is subject to section 362's automatic stay.[27]

Take a simple example: Bogartco has its checking account, with a $2 million balance, at Falcon State Bank. The bank has also lent Bogartco $10 million. Upon bankruptcy, Falcon State Bank can petition the court to allow it to setoff the two obligations – the bank account is a debt owed to Bogartco by the bank, and that can be paired with the loan between the same two parties.[28] Upon court approval of the setoff, Bogartco's bank account goes away, and its liability to the bank is reduced to $8 million.

---

[24] United Sav. Ass'n of Texas v. Timbers of Inwood Forest Assocs., Ltd., 484 U.S. 365, 382 (1988).

[25] Citizens Bank of Md. v. Strumpf, 516 U.S. 16, 18 (1995) (quoting Studley v. Boylston Nat'l Bank, 229 U.S. 523, 528 (1913)).

[26] In re Orexigen Therapeutics Inc., 18-10518 (Bankr. D. Del. Nov. 13, 2018).

[27] A setoff completed pre-petition is subject to a special preference rule within § 553 that, like § 547, looks to see if the setoff allowed the non-debtor party to receive more than they would have in bankruptcy.

[28] But if the loan was between the bank and Bogartco's Nova Scotian subsidiary, the setoff would fail, because there would be no "mutuality" of parties. That is, Bogartco's subsidiary is not Bogartco itself, and the introduction of a third party into the mix thwarts the setoff. This is discussed further below.

The rules and limitations on setoff do not apply to a creditor's right of "recoupment," although many attorneys have trouble keeping setoff and recoupment distinct. It is probably best to think of recoupment as a narrow form of setoff, that only applies when the setoff in question arises from the very same transaction as the creditor's claim against the debtor.[29] Most disputes over whether a particular setoff is actually a case of recoupment turn on the question of whether the facts involve the "same transaction."

Imagine Bogartco hires a contractor to remodel its offices. In the process of doing the remodeling, the contractor breaks several windows. Whoops.

If the contractor is unpaid when Bogartco files for bankruptcy, it will be able to use recoupment to reduce its outstanding claim against Bogartco. Bascially, the cost of the window replacement will be offset against the unpaid bill from Bogartco, without any need to petition the bankruptcy court. But if the contractor was unpaid by Bogartco on this job, and overpaid on an earlier job, that will be a setoff subject to the rules of 553 and the automatic stay.

As the First Circuit has explained, "[a] setoff is C's deduction from C's debt to B of an amount based on B's unrelated debt to C; a recoupment is C's deduction from C's debt to B based on B's debt to C arising out of the same transaction."[30]

A key aspect of setoff under section 553 is the requirement that there must be a "debt owing by such creditor to the debtor that arose before the commencement of the case under this title" against which the creditor may setoff its claim. And the creditor's claim and the debt against which the creditor seeks to exercise a right of setoff must be "mutual" obligations. That is, the two offsetting debts might be between the exact same parties. Different legal entities, even within the same corporate group do not count: the same party requirement is applied strictly – that is, it must be the *exact* same parties.[31]

---

[29]   In re Drexel Burnham Lambert Grp., Inc., 113 B.R. 830, 853 (Bankr. S.D.N.Y. 1990).

[30]   In re Slater Health Ctr., Inc., 398 F.3d 98, 103 (1st Cir. 2005).

[31]   In re SemCrude, L.P., 399 B.R. 388, 393-94 (Bankr. D. Del. 2009). The exception is that the U.S. government is considered a "unitary creditor" for purposes of meeting the mutuality requirement under section 553(a), even if the claims at issue involve more than one part of the government.

DISTRIBUTIONS TO CREDITORS

After creditors have filed their claims and the court has ruled on all objections, the claims are paid. In chapter 7, claims are paid according to the statute, in chapter 11, according to the terms of the plan (which must, of course, comply with the statute).

We will come back to payment when we discuss the respective chapters.

But the basic payout rules start with the proposition that secured creditors take first, or, more precisely, that allowed secured claims – that is, secured claims up to the value of the underlying collateral – get paid in full, before all others. They might receive this value over a long period of time, but they are entitled to receive the full value of their collateral before any value goes to other parties.

Finding a direct citation for this in the Bankruptcy Code is difficult – more often, "secured creditors first," seems to come down to bankruptcy lore.[32] But we can find some basis for this in section 541(a)(1), which provides that the estate is composed of "all legal or equitable interests of the debtor in property as of the commencement of the case." By implication, the estate does not include a secured creditor's interests in the debtor's property, and thus, if the debtor wants to keep the property after bankruptcy, free of the creditor's rights, it has to pay for it. Otherwise the lender gets its collateral back.[33]

Unsecured creditors are then paid. First, those who have a priority under section 507 are paid, and then all other creditors.[34] Only if there are sufficient funds to pay each level of priority claims, in order, will the general unsecured creditors receive any recovery. In many business liquidation cases under chapter 7, there is not even enough to pay all the rungs of priority claims.[35]

However, if there is anything left after paying all the creditors, this residue goes to the shareholders or other owners of the

---

[32] A few state laws are clearer – *e.g.*, HAW. REV. STAT. § 667-3 – but frequently this is just something that "everybody knows."

[33] Bankruptcy Code § 725.

[34] Bankruptcy Code §§ 507(a), 726. *See* Chapter 9.

[35] *See generally* Stephen J. Lubben, *Business Liquidation*, 81 AM. BANKR. L.J. 65 (2007).

business.[36] More precisely, the estate pays it to the debtor, who can then distribute it to the equity under state law rules.

The chapter 7 payout rules are a baseline. As we will see, chapter 11 plans are free to deviate from this structure, provided the debtor obtains the requisite consent of its creditors.

As a general rule, in a chapter 11 case, most holders of priority unsecured claims must receive payment in full in cash, unless the holder of a particular priority unsecured claim agrees to different treatment or the class accepts a chapter 11 plan that provides for deferred cash payments equal to the allowed amount of such claim.[37] General unsecured claims in a chapter 11 plan are distributed *pro rata* from the assets left after distributions are made to the priority unsecured claims.

It is also important to realize that the onset of bankruptcy changes the incentives to litigate many of these issues. Specifically, a fight over $10,000 outside of bankruptcy is a fight over $1,000 in a case that pays ten cents on the dollar and that changes the incentives to object to or file claims in the first place.

Sometimes it's easiest to think of these reduced payments in bankruptcy as involving "bankruptcy dollars" – as different from "regular" dollars as Canadian Dollars are from US Dollars. Once the debt gets converted into bankruptcy dollars, the currency of payment in bankruptcy courts, the effects on parties' incentives can be substantial.

SUMMARY

In a prior Chapter, we saw how the commencement of a bankruptcy estate creates an estate. In this Chapter, we examined how creditors can present their claims to the estate for payment. In particular, a creditor has to file a proof of claim, and work through the process of getting its claim "allowed." Once allowed, the claim will entitle the creditor to participate in the bankruptcy process, as we will explore in upcoming chapters. We will also learn how certain

---

[36] Bankruptcy Code § 726(a)(6).
[37] Bankruptcy Code § 1129(a)(9)(B). *See* Chapter 16.

administrative claims – which we say, get paid with a first priority among unsecured claims – are created.

5. Executory contracts and unexpired leases

Key concepts:

- Rejection as breach
- Assumption as performance
- The power to assign
- "Executory" contracts
- Chapter 11 and collective bargaining agreements

When a company enters bankruptcy, it commonly owes money to many, many different creditors. But it will also be party to many ongoing contracts, which have the character of both debts and assets.[1] That is, a contract might require Bogartco to pay $1 million for a truck full of felt, but Bogartco needs that felt to keep manufacturing fedoras.

Section 365 allows the debtor or trustee to sift through these contracts and decide which ones to keep or "assume."[2] The rest will be breached – or "rejected," in bankruptcy speak – and dealt with as all other pre-petition debts are dealt with. That is, the Code gives the trustee the power to breach a contract after bankruptcy, but treat it as if it were breached just before the petition was filed.[3]

As Justice Kagan recently summarized:

---

[1]   *See* Mission Prod. Holdings, Inc. v. Tempnology, LLC, No. 17-1657, 2019 WL 2166392, at *2 (U.S. May 20, 2019) ("Such an agreement represents both an asset (the debtor's right to the counterparty's future performance) and a liability (the debtor's own obligations to perform).").

[2]   Throughout § 365, the Code references "executory contract or unexpired lease." Save when the distinction is important, I simply use "contract" throughout this Chapter, except where the distinction between lease and contract is relevant.

[3]   Bankruptcy Code § 365(g)(1). *See also* Bankruptcy Code § 502(g)(1).

Section 365(a) enables the debtor (or its trustee), upon entering bankruptcy, to decide whether the contract is a good deal for the estate going forward. If so, the debtor will want to assume the contract, fulfilling its obligations while benefiting from the counterparty's performance. But if not, the debtor will want to reject the contract, repudiating any further performance of its duties. The bankruptcy court will generally approve that choice, under the deferential "business judgment" rule.[4]

In chapter 7 cases, any contracts not assumed are automatically rejected after sixty days.[5] In chapter 11, the debtor generally can wait until the court approves its reorganization plan, but another provision of the Code requires the debtor to address its non-residential real property leases within 120 days of the commencement of the case, although the court has the power to extend this period another ninety days.[6] That means that a debtor with many leases – perhaps a chain of retail stores – will need to decide which leases it wants to keep very early in the case, perhaps even before it can negotiate a plan with its creditors.[7] If possible, the debtor will want to begin this planning before even filing its bankruptcy petition.

Any decision by the debtor to assume or reject a contract is subject to court approval. The debtor or trustee must move for authorization to assume or reject, on notice to other creditors.

As noted, any contracts that the debtor or trustee wants to keep can be "assumed." The trustee can also assume and then assign most contracts, which means that valuable deals that the debtor no longer needs can be preserved and sold, generating return for all creditors.[8]

Assumption is the Code's term for agreeing to perform on the contract. If the debtor wants to assume a contract, it must cure any past defaults and make a credible promise to perform going

---

[4] *Mission Product Holdings*, 2019 WL 2166392, at *2.
[5] Bankruptcy Code § 365(d)(1).
[6] Bankruptcy Code § 365(d)(4).
[7] Before the 2005 amendments to the Code, the court had the power to extend the § 365(d)(4) deadline repeatedly, and generally did so in chapter 11 cases.
[8] If they were instead breached, or rejected, the benefit of the new contract would go to the non-debtor counterparty. Section 365's assumption and assignment powers can thus be seen as another part of the collectiveness of bankruptcy.

forward.[9] The effect of curing the defaults is that the counterparty to an assumed contract is likely to get better treatment than general unsecured creditors, who are rarely paid in full.

Before a contract can be assigned, the debtor or trustee must assume it. The ability to assume and assign generally exists even if the contract prohibits assignment, or purports to terminate upon a bankruptcy filing.[10] But the ability to assume or assign is partially limited by section 365(c).

That provision clearly prohibits the assignment of loans and personal service contracts. More generally, subsection (c) prevents the assignment of contracts where the identity of the parties is key, and which would generally be non-assignable under state law.

The effect of section 365(c) on the assumption of a contract by the debtor, particularly in a chapter 11 reorganization case where the debtor acts as trustee, is a bit fuzzier. In particular, can the debtor assume a contract as part of its own reorganization when section 365(c) would prohibit the assignment of such a contract?

On the one hand, some courts hold that the literal language of the section prohibits any assumption of a non-assignable contract.[11] This would prevent the debtor from assuming a personal services contract, even though, after assumption, the parties to the contract would be the same.[12] On the other hand, many bankruptcy courts, and at least one Court of Appeal, have held such a strict reading of

---

[9]   Bankruptcy Code § 365(b). In re Thane Int'l, Inc., No. 15-12186 (KG), 2018 WL 1027658, at *7 (Bankr. D. Del. Feb. 21, 2018).

[10]   Bankruptcy Code §§ 365(e), (f).

[11]   "The trustee may not assume or assign any executory contract or unexpired lease of the debtor ... if ... applicable law excuses a party ... to such contract or lease from accepting performance from or rendering performance to an entity other than the debtor or the debtor in possession." The literal language of § 365(c)(1) is thus said to put forth a "hypothetical test:" a debtor may not assume an executory contract over the non-debtor's objection if applicable law would bar assignment to a third party, even where the debtor in possession has no intention of assigning the contract in question to a third party.

[12]   In re Catapult Entertainment, Inc., 165 F.3d 747 (9th Cir. 1999). This reading has been adopted by a majority of the other Courts of Appeals that have addressed this question. In re Sunterra Corp., 361 F.3d 257 (4th Cir. 2004); In re James Cable Partners, L. P., 27 F.3d 534 (11th Cir. 1994) (per curiam); In re West Electronics, Inc., 852 F.2d 79 (3d Cir. 1988).

the text to be inane.[13] Whatever the statute might seem to say, it would make horrible policy to read it that way.

Until the Supreme Court weighs in – or Congress clarifies – the issue remains uncertain, and the divergent case law undoubtedly contributes to the "forum shopping" we discussed in Chapter 2. If the debtor's business depends on a licensing agreement, for example, why would its counsel ever recommend filing in a jurisdiction that would prohibit assumption of the agreement?

The powers given to a debtor or trustee by section 365 are sometimes described as extraordinary, almost super-human.[14] But really the ability to reject or assume are just the bankruptcy law equivalents of the ability to breach or perform, something every contractual counterparty has. The fact that the party to a rejected contract will not receive full payment is more a function of the debtor's insolvency than any special feature of the Code.[15]

One bit of "magic" in section 365 is found in section 365(g), which moves the breach of a contract from post-petition to pre-petition. That shift in timing gives the debtor the breathing space to figure out what it wants to do with its business. But in all other respects, the effect of rejection under section 365 should be just the same as if the debtor had breached the contract right before filing its bankruptcy petition. Rather modest magic.

The assumption power does not change anything, save for giving the debtor a small ability to make up for past sins by curing

---

[13] Institut Pasteur v. Cambridge Biotech Corp., 104 F.3d 489, 493 (1st Cir. 1997). *See also* In re Mirant Corp., 440 F.3d 238, 248-49 (5th Cir. 2006); In re Cumberland Corral, LLC, No. 313-06325, 2014 Bankr. LEXIS 936, at *23 (Bankr. M.D. Tenn. Mar. 11, 2014).

[14] Much of the difficulty here turns on courts' tendency to frame rejection as inevitably resulting in a claim against the estate, with no other outcome (such as continued possession) seemingly possible. In re Tempnology, LLC, 879 F.3d 389, 392 (1st Cir. 2018) ("Generally speaking, when a company files for protection under Chapter 11 of the Bankruptcy Code, the trustee or the debtor-in-possession may secure court approval to 'reject' any executory contract of the debtor, meaning that the other party to the contract is left with a damages claim for breach, but not the ability to compel further performance."), *reversed and remanded by* Mission Product Holdings, Inc. v. Tempnology, LLC, U.S., May 20, 2019.

[15] *See generally* Stephen J. Lubben, *Derivatives and Bankruptcy: The Flawed Case for Special Treatment*, 12 U. PA. J. BUS. L. 61 (2009).

defaults.[16] Otherwise if the debtor wants to treat the contract as an asset, it has to perform.[17]

The assignment power contains the other deviation from non-bankruptcy law, to the extent it allows assignment of contracts with otherwise enforceable anti-assignment provisions.[18] This is consistent with other provisions of the Code that prevent a non-debtor counterparty from realizing a windfall or otherwise extracting themselves from the collective bankruptcy process.[19]

The Code respects restrictions on assignments where the law advances legitimate policy goals – such as with regard to the traditional rule against assigning personal service contracts. Where the Bankruptcy Code does change the underlying law is with regard to anti-assignment provisions that represent little more than an attempt to undermine the Code's preference for creditor equality. An anti-assignment provision without any underlying policy goal is really no more than an attempt by the counterparty to grab an inequitable share of the debtor's assets as the price of consent to the assignment.

One area of general confusion with regard to section 365 turns on the Code's use of the phrase "executory contract," rather than simply "contract." On the one hand, this could be interpreted to simply mean that the assumption and rejection powers only apply to contracts that are still "alive," because contracts that are over and done with are really more claims than contracts. This was recently suggested by the Supreme Court, when it proclaimed that "[s]ection 365 of the Bankruptcy Code enables a debtor to 'reject any executory contract'—meaning a contract that neither party has finished performing."[20] As the leading textbook summarizes, under

---

[16]   Bankruptcy Code § 365(b).

[17]   As summarized by Vern Countryman:

[I]f [the trustee or debtor] wants the other party's performance, [the trustee or debtor] must render the performance due from the bankrupt. Hence, if the trustee assumes the contract, the other party's claims under it become first priority administration expenses. At this point, then, the other contracting party is in a better position than he [or she] was prior to bankruptcy.

Vern Countryman, *The Use of State Law in Bankruptcy Cases (Part I)*, 47 N.Y.U. L. REV. 407, 415 (1972).

[18]   Bankruptcy Code § 365(f).

[19]   *E.g.*, Bankruptcy Code §§ 365(e), 541(c).

[20]   *Mission Prod. Holdings*, 2019 WL 2166392, at *2.

this understanding "the executoriness doctrine means nothing more than that if a contract is fully performed or terminated before bankruptcy, the trustee gets no special powers under §365."[21] But many courts have instead held that the requirement of "executoriness" does some real work in screening which agreements can be subject to section 365.[22]

Largely drawing on a series of law review articles written to address questions under the old Bankruptcy Act, these courts apply the "Countryman" test of executoriness.[23] This test provides that a contract is executory only when the failure of *either* party to perform would constitute a *material* breach. Under this test, each party must have considerable unperformed duties remaining before section 365 applies.[24]

As a result, the courts have struggled with contracts where one party performs up front, while the other performs in the future.[25] Perhaps more generally, we might suspect that courts are uncomfortable with the option that section 365 gives the debtor, and the use of executoriness represents an attempt to cabin the 365 power.

Some of the confusion also seems to come from the tendency to vest section 365 with superpowers, as we noted earlier. For example, rejection of a contract is often treated as if the contract was vaporized upon rejection.[26] The better approach is to consider what the consequences of breach are under non-bankruptcy law, and apply those same consequences to rejection under section 365,

---

[21] ELIZABETH WARREN ET AL., THE LAW OF DEBTORS AND CREDITORS 577 (7TH ED. 2014).

[22] *See, e.g.*, In re Baird, 567 F.3d 1207, 1211 (10th Cir. 2009); In re Liljeberg Enters., 304 F.3d 410, 436 (5th Cir. 2002); In re Columbia Gas Sys. Inc., 50 F.3d 233, 239 (3d Cir. 1995).

[23] *E.g.*, Vern Countryman, *Executory Contracts in Bankruptcy, Part 1*, 57 MINN. L. REV. 439, 460 (1973).

[24] For a clearly explained application of the Countryman test, see In re Cho, 581 B.R. 452, 461-66 (Bankr. D. Md. 2018).

[25] In corporate finance, these would be called forward contracts.

[26] *See, e.g.*, in Lubrizol Enters., Inc. v. Richmond Metal Finishers, Inc. (In re Richmond Metal Finishers Inc.), 756 F.2d 1043 (4th Cir. 1985). In *Lubrizol*, the court held that, if a debtor rejects an executory IP license, the licensee loses all right to use any licensed copyrights, trademarks, and patents, and its sole remedy is a pre-petition breach claim. The Supreme Court recently rejected *Lubrizol*'s analysis of section 365 in *Mission Product Holdings*, 2019 WL 2166392, at *7 (U.S. May 20, 2019).

unless there is some bankruptcy policy that should override that result.[27] "Executoriness" plays no role in the analysis.

The Supreme Court adopted this approach to rejection in its recent holding in *Mission Product Holdings*, where it explained

> According to one view, a rejection has the same consequence as a contract breach outside bankruptcy: It gives the counterparty a claim for damages, while leaving intact the rights the counterparty has received under the contract. According to the other view, a rejection (except in a few spheres) has more the effect of a contract rescission in the non-bankruptcy world: Though also allowing a damages claim, the rejection terminates the whole agreement along with all rights it conferred. Today, we hold that both Section 365's text and fundamental principles of bankruptcy law command the first, rejection-as-breach approach … *Rejection of a contract—any contract—in bankruptcy operates not as a rescission but as a breach.*[28]

In cases where state contract law provides for payment of expectation damages, the "vaporization" (or rescission) approach is overstated, but largely harmless. The contract is replaced with a claim for the payment of money. But in some cases, the non-breaching party might have an equitable remedy, because money damages are not sufficient to make them whole. These cases do not really work with the "vaporization" concept, because under state law the non-debtor counterparty may end up controlling the subject matter of the contract, even after breach-rejection.

For example, if I enter into a contract to buy an apartment, and the seller then files bankruptcy, under state law I probably can demand transfer of the apartment, rather than money damages. Under the Countryman approach, courts will spend a lot of time worrying about whether this contract is still executory – what if I have already paid the purchase price into escrow? – and thus subject to section 365. Probably the better focus would be whether the apartment is fully part of the bankruptcy estate under section 541, or whether the debtor only has something like legal title, while I have an equitable interest in the place.[29]

---

[27]   *See generally* Jay Lawrence Westbrook & Kelsi Stayart White, *The Demystification of Contracts in Bankruptcy*, 91 AM. BANKR. L.J. 481 (2017).

[28]   *Mission Product Holdings*, 2019 WL 2166392, at *5 (emphasis added).

[29]   Some might argue that by only giving a lien to a purchaser who has paid under § 365(j), Congress intended to override state law that gives the buyer

That is, "a debtor's rejection of an executory contract in bank-ruptcy has the same effect as a breach outside bankruptcy. Such an act cannot rescind rights that the contract previously granted."[30] The question is not whether the agreement is "executory," but what the effects of breach of such a contract would be outside of bankruptcy.

Limited liability company or LLC agreements are another source of endless confusion in this area. If a debtor is an investor in an LLC, it holds two things at the petition date: a membership interest, which undoubtedly comes into the estate, and rights under an operating agreement, which, among other things, sets forth the entitlements conferred to the holder of the membership interest. In some sense the two – membership interest and operating agreement – are inseparable, because neither really works without the other.

Nonetheless, courts spend an inordinate amount of time worrying about whether the operating agreement is subject to section 365, a question that becomes particularly trying under the Countryman test if the debtor is a passive investor in the LLC.[31] The debtor's performance consisted of delivering over a lump of cash or other assets at the outset of the investment. Finding a *material* breach in the remaining bits of performance – often voting rights and maybe some vague obligation to participate in governance – becomes a bit of a stretch.

But if the operating agreement does not fall within the trustee or debtor's powers to assume, is the contract in or out of the estate? And does the debtor still have an ownership interest in the LLC, even if the operating agreement has "gone away"? The question of executoriness would be an irrelevant diversion if the courts treated the (non-executory) operating agreements as assets of the estate, but in some cases courts go on to say that section 365(e)'s prohibition on enforcement of bankruptcy termination clauses – so called *ipso facto* clauses, as aficionados of the Roman Empire are sure to call them – does not apply to "non-executory" contracts.[32] Many LLC

---

equitable title without possession and therefore access to specific performance. There does not appear to be any case law on the question of whether § 365(j) preempts all other remedies for the non-breaching party, and whether Congress can constitutionally destroy equitable title to property. But these issues, while interest-ing, are far beyond the scope of this introductory text.

[30]   *Mission Product Holdings*, 2019 WL 2166392, at *9.

[31]   In re Tsiaoushis, 383 B.R. 616, 620 (Bankr. E.D. Va. 2007).

[32]   Id. at 621. The court does not address Bankruptcy Code § 541(c)(1)(B).

operating agreements purport to terminate on the bankruptcy of a member; others may provide for the bankrupt member to be involuntarily "bought out" by the remaining members or the LLC itself.

Arguably the better analysis would be to assume that contracts that have not fully run their course are subject to section 365, and move on to the question of whether the operating agreement can be assigned, if relevant.

The trustee or debtor should have the choice of assuming or rejecting the agreement, without having to worry about bankruptcy triggering termination, but if the agreement is to be assigned, state law (and common law, for that matter) that prohibits the introduction of strangers into a partnership without the consent of all partners would seem to be relevant to the analysis under Bankruptcy Code section 365(c).[33] The court should also consider if there is some good bankruptcy policy that would justify overriding state partnership law on this point.

Most every scholar would abandon the Countryman test because it is confusing and not consistent with the purpose of bankruptcy law. Nevertheless, until the Supreme Court weighs in on the specific issue of "executoriness"[34] or Congress acts, a sizable number of courts will continue to apply that test. What happens after determining that a contract is not sufficiently executory is too often left vague, and the contract then enters into a kind of purgatory where it is neither asset nor claim.

Another interesting wrinkle in the Code's treatment of contracts comes in chapter 11, where collective bargaining agreements – such as those between a debtor-firm and a union – are subject to special rules.[35] The story here begins with the Supreme Court's decision in

---

[33] *See* In re Ionosphere Clubs, Inc., 85 F.3d 992, 998–99 (2d Cir. 1996).

[34] The Court's recent decision in *Mission Product Holdings* did not directly address the putative threshold issue of "executoriness," although the Court did embrace the *Bildisco* definition of an executory contract as one where "performance remains due to some extent on both sides." *Mission Product Holdings*, 2019 WL 2166392, at *2 (*quoting* NLRB v. Bildisco & Bildisco, 465 U.S. 513, 522, n. 6 (1984)), which the Court restated as "meaning a contract that neither party has finished performing." *Id.* This suggests something less than the Countryman test would require, but would still require some remaining performance on both sides, and again the issue was not directly before the Court.

[35] Bankruptcy Code § 1113.

NLRB v. Bildisco & Bildisco, where the court suggested some loose guidelines for the debtor's rejection of a collective bargaining agreement.[36] The Supreme Court further held that it is not an unfair labor practice – under federal labor law – for a debtor to unilaterally breach a collective bargaining agreement before its rejection.

Congress added section 1113 to the Code in response to *Bildisco*.[37] By and large, the provision codifies the Court's first holding, that provides that rejection of a collective bargaining agreement is not subject to the normal rules, and the debtor has to show "something more" to reject a union contract.

But the main response to *Bildisco* can be found in section 1113(f), which provides that no provision of the Code "shall be construed to permit a trustee to unilaterally terminate or alter any provisions of a collective bargaining agreement prior to compliance with the provisions of this section." In short, Congress rejected the second part of the Court's holding, and debtors in chapter 11 have to comply with federal labor law until they actually reject their collective bargaining agreements – no "head starts."

Note that because section 1113 is codified within chapter 11, it only applies in that chapter, and would not apply in a business chapter 7 case.[38] Presumably the trustee will habitually reject the collective bargaining agreement in most chapter 7 cases, because the business is liquidating.

To similar effect is section 1114, again a "chapter 11 only" provision.[39] Section 1114 was enacted, along with section 1129(a)(13) of the Code, as part of the Retiree Benefits Bankruptcy Protection Act of 1988 ("RBBPA"). RBBPA was enacted in direct response to actions taken by LTV Corporation, which, in 1986, filed

---

[36] The story of the case is told in one chapter of RONALD J. MANN, BANKRUPTCY AND THE U.S. SUPREME COURT (2017).

[37] Congress has enacted special statutory provisions for specific types of executory contracts in several instances, such as §§ 365(n) (intellectual property licenses), 1113 (collective bargaining agreements), 1110 (aircraft leases) and 1169 (railroad lines).

[38] Or a municipal chapter 9 bankruptcy case.

[39] Bankruptcy Code § 1114.

for bankruptcy and then immediately moved under section 365 of the Code to terminate benefits for thousands of retired employees.[40]

Under section 1114, only after good faith negotiations with retirees' appointed representatives have failed can the debtor apply to the bankruptcy court to modify retiree benefits. The debtor has the burden of showing that the proposed modifications are necessary to facilitate its reorganization.[41]

SUMMARY

Contracts and leases have the character of both assets and liabilities. Section 365 of the Code gives the trustee the ability to convert all of the debtor's "bad" contracts into claims against the estate. That is, the trustee can breach the agreements, effective as of the petition date. The trustee also has the power to perform or assume the "good" contracts. Good contracts that the debtor is unable to perform itself can be assigned in many cases to a party that can perform. The broadened ability to assign contracts generates value for the estate, and is consistent with the communal exercise that is business bankruptcy.

---

[40] Congress twice passed stop-gap legislation forcing LTV to continue to pay retiree benefits while the RBBPA was being drafted and debated. *See generally* In re Visteon Corp., 612 F.3d 210, 216-229 (3d Cir. 2010).

[41] A split has developed among the circuits as to whether a debtor must adhere to section 1114 even when it has a prepetition contractual right to modify or terminate retiree benefit plans. Another reason to carefully consider venue, as discussed in Chapter 2.

6. The avoidance powers

Key concepts:

- Avoidable preferences
- Fraudulent transfers
- Trustee exercising the powers of existing unsecured creditors
- Trustee exercising the powers of a lien creditor and bona fide purchaser

---

As we noted in Chapter 3, every bankruptcy case involves a bankruptcy estate, tended to by a trustee.[1] The Code gives the trustee various rights and powers, some of which are collectively referred to as the avoidance or avoiding powers. These powers foster equal treatment among creditors, by defeating any pre-bankruptcy creditor (or debtor) efforts to drain assets out of the debtor, and thus the estate. This Chapter focuses on three of the central avoiding powers: the preference provisions, the fraudulent transfer provisions, and the trustee's "strong arm" provisions.

PREFERENCES UNDER SECTION 547

A preference is a payment or other transfer to a creditor,[2] made on the eve of bankruptcy, that allows the creditor to get a greater recovery on its claim than other creditors.

---

[1]   Or the debtor in chapter 11, as will be discussed in Chapter 11.

[2]   The Code defines "transfer" in § 101(54) to include the creation of liens and involuntary transfers. Receiving any interest in property qualifies as a transfer, which means that taking a security interest or recording that interest to perfect it against other creditors qualifies as a transfer. Obtaining additional collateral under an existing security interest would also be covered. Determination of whether a "transfer" has occurred is separate from determination of *when* the transfer

More formally, section 547(b) of the Bankruptcy Code defines a preference as:

- a payment of an "antecedent" (preexisting) debt;
- made while the debtor was insolvent (*i.e.*, its assets were less than its liabilities[3]);
- within 90 days of filing bankruptcy (or one year for transfers to insiders[4])

that allows the creditor to receive more on its claim than it would have, if the claim was instead paid in the bankruptcy proceeding.

This last requirement gets fully secured creditors off the hook, since they are entitled to receive the value of their collateral first, as we discussed back in Chapter 4. The limitation of preferences to transfers on preexisting debts also means when the debtor obtains a loan from a bank and simultaneously gives a security interest in its assets to secure the obligation there will be no preference.[5]

But otherwise, the question of whether a transfer permits a creditor to receive more than it would in liquidation is typically fairly simple, because in many cases the creditor received full payment before bankruptcy: if a liquidation would result in anything less than full payment of all claims, the transfer to an unsecured creditor always permits that creditor to receive more than it would have received in liquidation. Similarly, a payment to a

---

occurred. Barnhill v. Johnson, 503 U.S. 393 (1992) (check resulted in transfer on date check was paid, not when it was written).

3   Bankruptcy Code § 101(32) defines "insolvent."

4   Bankruptcy Code § 101(31) defines the term "insider." The term includes certain specified relatives (for individuals) and directors, officers, other agents, and affiliates (for business entities). But the key word in the definition is "includes" because it makes clear that the statutory list is not exclusive. As Justice Kagan recently explained:

> Courts have additionally recognized as insiders some persons not on that list—commonly known as "non-statutory insiders." The conferral of that status often turns on whether the person's transactions with the debtor (or another of its insiders) were at arm's length.

U.S. Bank N.A. v. Vill. at Lakeridge, LLC, 138 S. Ct. 960, 962 (2018).

5   *See also* Bankruptcy Code § 547(c)(1). The cited exception covers *nearly* simultaneous exchanges. A truly contemporaneous exchange, such as the transfer of goods for cash or the transfer of a loan for security interest, is not a voidable preference because there is no antecedent debt.

partially secured creditor reduces the unsecured portion of the overall claim first, since the security interest remains in effect to cover the balance of the debt, and the creditor is also receiving more than it would have received in liquidation.

Imagine two trade creditors, both of whom are getting nervous, because Bogartco has not paid their invoices. The first creditor phones up the president, HB, and threatens to sue if she does not get paid. HB tells the finance department to pay the bill. A week later, Bogartco files for bankruptcy. Without section 547, the first creditor would be able retain its payment and be paid in full, and the second creditor would get whatever creditors get in the bankruptcy case – often just pennies on the dollar. But because the first creditor's payment is subject to avoidance and recovery under section 547, it is left to the same fate as creditor number two – it will receive the same distribution. In essence, we have equalized their payouts.

Without section 547, the second creditor is smart and will threaten to file a lawsuit before the first creditor. The first creditor is smart too, and knows the second creditor will do this, making the first creditor call all the sooner. And, so on and so forth ... and you have the race to the courthouse.

The preference provision potentially deters "runs" on the debtor on the eve of bankruptcy. Not only does this promote creditor equality, but it potentially avoids creditor action that tips a company into an unnecessary bankruptcy filing. And note that there is no element of intent here: the perfectly innocent creditor who receives a preference will still have to return it.

Preference recoveries are not automatic. Section 547 simply defines "preference." Section 550 of the Bankruptcy Code allows the trustee to recover any preferential payment (or other avoidable payment) by filing a lawsuit against the creditor.

Sections 547 and 550 notwithstanding, creditors are almost always better off attempting to get payment before bankruptcy and dealing with the possible preference liability later. The debtor may not file bankruptcy, in which case there would be no liability. And many factors can influence the trustee's decision whether to sue to recover a preference. Accordingly, the "deterrent" effect of sections 547 and 550 may be only potential.[6]

PREFERENCE DEFENSES

Section 547 also contains several built-in defenses to a preference action, beyond the inherent defense of showing that some element – for example, perhaps the debtor was solvent[7] – was not present.[8] For example, payments of debts in the ordinary course of business – measured either subjectively or objectively, through industry practice – are not preferences.[9] Thus, creditor number one, in our earlier example, might be able to show that Bogartco always paid only when threatened, and thus get out of any obligation to return the payment.[10] Maybe.

The new value defense to preferences, under section 547(c)(4) of the Code, applies where the creditor provided new value (such as shipping goods or providing services) to the debtor after a preference.[11] In other words, if a creditor ships new goods after an alleged preferential transfer is made, the value of those goods or services can be subtracted from the preferential transfer on a dollar-for-dollar basis. The new exposure to the debtor offsets the creditor's prior receipt of a preference.[12]

---

[6]   Preference provisions also equalize the distribution among creditors by reducing the power of old management to choose the creditors that get paid and the ones that do not.

[7]   Bankruptcy Code § 547(f) includes a presumption the debtor was *insolvent* ninety days before bankruptcy, meaning the creditor must prove otherwise. For the one-year reach-back against insiders, the presumption of insolvency only runs for the ninety days immediately preceding filing; thereafter, the trustee or debtor will be required to prove insolvency.

[8]   Bankruptcy Code § 547(c) provides nine separate defenses that a creditor can assert to defeat a preference claim.

[9]   Bankruptcy Code § 547(c)(2).

[10]   But some courts have ruled that paying in response to creditor pressure can never be paying the "ordinary course." In re Valley Food Servs., LLC, 389 B.R. 685, 690 (Bankr. W.D. Mo. 2008).

[11]   New value is defined in § 547(a)(2) of the Code as "money or money's worth in goods, services or new credit ... ."

[12]   Accordingly, the new value has to be unsecured, otherwise the creditor has no real exposure.

The Code also excludes attempts to recover small preferences – $6,825 at present.[13] Essentially Congress has decided that it is inherently inefficient to allow trustees to recover such small amounts, perhaps given the likelihood that the creditor would spend more than that amount defending against such an action.

FRAUDULENT (OR "VOIDABLE") TRANSFERS

Preferential transfers should not be confused with fraudulent transfers or fraudulent conveyances.[14] Though they are often lumped together, they are distinct concepts. A preferential transfer focuses on whether a creditor has received a payment that results in that creditor getting better treatment than other creditors in the bankruptcy. A fraudulent transfer, on the other hand, looks at whether an insolvent entity has made a transfer to another party (perhaps a creditor, but maybe not) for which the insolvent entity did not receive real value in return.

Every state has its own fraudulent conveyance or transfer law, which is applicable outside bankruptcy as well as in bankruptcy. As we will discuss further below, section 544 codifies several "strong arm" trustee powers. Of relevance here is section 544(b), in which the trustee is given the powers of individual creditors, to use them for the good of whole estate. The trustee may avoid any transfer "that is voidable under applicable law by a creditor holding an unsecured claim." In addition, the Bankruptcy Code contains its own fraudulent conveyance law, in section 548 of the Code, which applies only in bankruptcy cases.

It is also worth noting that state fraudulent transfer law is in the process of being renamed, although I will continue to refer to "fraudulent transfers" from here on out. The most up to date state laws in this area are based on the "Uniform Voidable Transactions Act."[15] The use of "fraud" in the names of the older statutes tended

---

[13]   This is one of those numbers that adjusts for inflation under § 104 of the Code. The next update will occur on April 1, 2022.

[14]   Fraudulent transfers or conveyances are the same thing, the latter being a somewhat older term for the former.

[15]   *E.g.*, CAL. CIV. CODE §§ 3439.01 *et seq.*

to lead to confusion among courts, and alarm amongst defendants.[16] Fraudulent transfers really have nothing to do with "fraud" in the tort sense of the word, and the new name (and a few new rules) aim to clear that up.

Whether under state or federal law, two broad types of fraudulent transfers can be undone. First, intentional fraudulent transfers are avoidable. These are transfers where the debtor attempts to "hinder, delay or defraud" its creditors. Imagine a court enters a large tort judgement against Bogartco, and twenty minutes later Bogartco decides to "gift" all of its assets to the newly formed "Humphreyco." A clear attempt to hinder collection of the tort judgment; the transfer can be unwound.

But what if instead of giving away its assets, Bogartco instead sells them to Humphreyco? If Bogartco sells for fair value, the creditors will not care, because Bogartco now has a pile of cash, and has saved the creditors the trouble of selling the assets themselves. But if our creditors think that Humphreyco has not paid enough for the assets, this might constitute a "constructive" fraudulent transfer.

This second type of fraudulent transfer occurs when a company transfers assets for less than "reasonably equivalent value."[17] So if Bogartco's assets are worth $1 million, but it sells them for $100,000, the tort creditors can undo this transaction, and get the assets back for sale at a proper price.

That is a pretty clear case, but state laws and the Bankruptcy Code, however, do not define "reasonably equivalent value." Courts tend to consider the issue in two parts: was there value, and, if so, was that value roughly comparable to what the debtor gave up in the deal?[18]

In the business bankruptcy context, it is important to remember that each company within a corporate group is a separate debtor – thus, a transfer from a parent company to a subsidiary, or a transfer

[16] Choice of law issues were often quite confused under UFTA as well.

[17] Bankruptcy Code § 548(a)(1)(B). The wording is slightly different under the state laws, but the effect is the same. For example, § 273 of the New York Debtor and Creditor Law provides that any conveyance made "without receiving a reasonably equivalent value in exchange for the transfer or obligation" is voidable.

[18] Bankruptcy Code § 548(d)(2)(A) provides a definition of "value" for these purposes.

by a subsidiary that benefits the parent company, might be subject to attack as a fraudulent transfer. For example, when a parent company received the proceeds of a loan, but the subsidiary grants a lien on its assets, we might ask if the subsidiary has received "reasonably equivalent value" in exchange for granting the lien.[19] If the parent company uses the loan proceeds to pay a large dividend to shareholders, what benefit did the corporation receive?[20]

A transfer without equality in value is only objectionable when the debtor is financially fragile, as measured by three possible tests.[21] One, whether the debtor was insolvent, is relatively definite,[22] but the other two – whether the debtor was left with unreasonably small capital or with debts beyond the debtor's ability to pay – are notable for their squishiness. Squishiness, of course, means litigation expenses.

Paying off an old debt constitutes receipt of reasonable value, although such payments may trigger scrutiny as a preference under section 547. Under section 548, a good faith transferee is given a lien against the property transferred to the extent it gave value.[23] Thus, Humphreyco will have to give Bogartco back its assets, but Humphreyco will be a secured creditor for the $100,000 it actually paid for those assets.

It is important to stress that constructive fraudulent transfers can be proven without any evidence of intent – fraudulent or otherwise.[24] The name "constructive fraudulent transfer" is more than a bit confusing in that regard. Hence the recent efforts to rename them.

---

[19] *See* In re Xonics Photochemical, Inc., 841 F.2d 198, 201 (7th Cir. 1988).

[20] Such a dividend might also be attacked under state corporate law, but that is not our focus here.

[21] Bankruptcy Code § 548(a)(1)(B)(ii).

[22] See the definition in Bankruptcy Code § 101(32)(A) ("financial condition such that the sum of such entity's debts is greater than all of such entity's property, at a fair valuation ...").

[23] Bankruptcy Code § 548(c).

[24] For example, under the UVTA in force in New York since 2020, a transfer for less than reasonable value is voidable simply if the debtor "was engaged or was about to engage in a business or a transaction for which the remaining assets of the debtor were unreasonably small in relation to the business or transaction." NEW YORK DEBTOR AND CREDITOR LAW § 273. Intent might become relevant if the trustee is trying to recover from transferees further down the chain of title. Bankruptcy Code § 550(b).

Transfers are avoidable under the Bankruptcy Code if made within two years of bankruptcy. Under the law of most states – and thus section 544(b) – transfers can be avoided if made within four years, but in some states (until recently New York) creditors and trustees can reach back six years.[25] Under section 544(b), however, the trustee has to act on behalf of an actual existing creditor. The creditor could be owed $1, but that creditor might have a right to bring the cause of action that the trustee will bring on behalf of all creditors. Under section 548, on the other hand, the trustee automatically has a right to avoid a transfer, even if no creditor would have standing to do so under state law.[26]

THE STRONG ARM CLAUSE

Section 544(a) of the Bankruptcy Code – commonly referred to as the "strong arm clause," although some include the previously

---

[25]   Rather than counting back from the petition date as in Bankruptcy Code section 548(a), state law generally counts forward from the date of the transaction. Nonetheless, in bankruptcy, the two limitation periods work the same, because the filing of a bankruptcy case will typically toll the running of the state limitation period, and a trustee then has the longer of two years or the length of the case in which to bring an action. Bankruptcy Code § 546(a). As one bankruptcy court has explained:

> The limitations period in § 546 is a double-edged sword for the trustee. If, at the beginning of a bankruptcy proceeding, a state-law fraudulent transfer claim is viable, then the trustee has two years to bring the claim—regardless of whether the claim is still viable under state law by the time the trustee brings the action. The § 546 limitations period usually operates to give the trustee "breathing room" to bring a claim even after the state-law limitations period has ended. But § 546 sometimes—as in this case—bars claims that would otherwise be viable under state law ... The Trustees here bring the claims under the authority of § 544, and they are bound by the limitations in § 546, regardless of what Texas law allows.

In re Juliet Homes, LP, Nos. 07-36424, 09-03429, 2010 Bankr. LEXIS 4826, at *50 (Bankr. S.D. Tex. Dec. 16, 2010).

[26]   In 2005, Congress added subclause (IV) to the constructively fraudulent transfer provision in § 548. Bankruptcy Code § 548(a)(1)(B)(ii)(IV). This provision has no state law counterpart, and allows non-ordinary course employment contracts to be undone by the debtor. Although the case law is sparse, it appears this provision applies without regard to the aforementioned conditions of financial fragility. That is, if the debtor grants a special bonus within two years of bankruptcy, that bonus might be challenged, even if the debtor was solvent.

discussed section 544(b) within that description – gives a bank-ruptcy trustee special powers to defeat certain creditors. It provides that "[t]he trustee shall have, as of the commencement of the case, and without regard to any knowledge of the trustee or of any creditor, the rights and powers of, or may avoid any transfer of property of the debtor or any obligation incurred by a debtor" that could have been invalidated by certain kinds of hypothetical judicial lienors, holders of unsatisfied executions or bona fide purchasers of real property.

Under the last power, the trustee has the same ability to acquire title to the debtor's assets as a purchaser who conducted a title search, paid value for the property and perfected her interest as a legal title holder as of the date of the commencement of the case.

Imagine the debtor has given a creditor a mortgage, but the creditor never bothered to record the mortgage in the property records, or mistakenly recorded it in the wrong place. An innocent purchaser of the property would take free of that mortgage, and thus so will the trustee. The creditor will become an unsecured creditor in the bankruptcy, and all will share in the proceeds of the would-be collateral.

Under section 544(a)(1), the trustee gets a kind of imaginary lien on all of the debtor's property, to the same extent that a judgment creditor could under state law. This again allows the trustee to defeat improperly created liens, albeit now against personal property. The broader purpose of the strong arm power is to cut off secret liens and other unknown claims to the debtor's assets, leaving the trustee free to advance the Bankruptcy Code's central goal of creditor equality.[27] Consistent with this, the trustee's ability to use the strong arm powers is independent of the trustee's actual knowledge of events. This can be especially important in chapter 11, where the trustee *is* the debtor.

---

[27] The strong arm powers are thus the bankruptcy counterpart to the powers the FDIC has in bank insolvency cases under the rule in the *D'Oench* case (which is now codified at 12 U.S.C. § 1823(e)). D'Oench, Duhme & Co. v. FDIC, 315 U.S. 447 (1942). The *D'Oench* doctrine, in short, provides that the FDIC is not subject to secret side agreements when marshalling a failed bank's assets.

SUMMARY

Preference actions avoid two problems: the debtor's management picking winners and losses on the eve of filing, and some creditors getting better treatment than others simply by virtue of when the petition is filed. Fraudulent transfer actions return assets to the estate that left either for inadequate value, or as part of the debtor's plot to hide its assets. And the strong arm powers allow the trustee to harness the powers of individual creditors for the benefit of the estate as a whole.

Some creditor collection actions that occurred before filing are honored, while others are set aside. The unifying theme in preference, fraudulent transfer, or strong arm actions is the protection of the estate against sharp practices that might benefit insiders at the expense of others. In many cases these rules will be overinclusive, but the aim is to protect the broad rule of creditor equality at relatively minor cost. Nonetheless, it is worth considering if the avoidance powers do not sometimes give a debtor or trustee too much power, particularly with regard to smaller creditors.

PART III

Liquidation under chapter 7

7. An introduction to chapter 7 of the Bankruptcy Code

Key concepts:

- An efficient general debt collection mechanism
- The 341 meeting
- Committees in chapter 7
- The shadow effect of chapter 7

Chapter 7 provides the procedure for the liquidation of insolvent companies (although, as we will see, liquidation can occur under chapter 11 as well).[1] In the United States, unlike most other jurisdictions,[2] an insolvent company has no legal obligation to commence insolvency proceedings, but the board's fiduciary duties, under general corporate law, demand that it do *something* to address financial distress. If the situation is truly hopeless, that something might be the company's liquidation under chapter 7. If the debtor fails to file voluntarily, creditors may file an involuntary chapter 7 petition (as discussed in Chapter 2).

Before we begin discussing chapter 7, it is worth noting that many small businesses will "liquidate" by simply failing to pay their franchise taxes, and waiting for the state government to suspend the corporation's charter. If necessary, the owner might file

---

[1] There are also a variety of state law alternatives to liquidation under the Bankruptcy Code. For a broad overview, see STEPHEN J. LUBBEN, THE LAW OF FAILURE: A TOUR THROUGH THE WILDS OF AMERICAN BUSINESS INSOLVENCY LAW (2018).

[2] Canada, like the United States, has no statutory restrictions on "trading while insolvent." Most every other jurisdiction does. *E.g.*, Helen Anderson, *Shelter from the Storm: Phoenix Activity and the Safe Harbour*, 41 MELB. U. L. REV. 999, 1002 (2018).

a personal bankruptcy case. A slightly more sophisticated version of this involves dissolving the company under state corporate law.[3]

But in some cases quarrels with creditors can be avoided by filing a chapter 7 case, and thus showing that the shareholders are not "hiding anything." That is, chapter 7 is used to signal transparency, because of the much more robust disclosure obligations under federal law.

Business entities do not receive a discharge in chapter 7.[4] Chapter 7 is thus best seen as a tool for winding up the company or a sale of the company as a going concern to new owners, but actual termination of the entity still has to happen under the state law that created the entity in the first instance.[5]

Chapter 7 is divided into five subchapters, the first two of which are generally applicable in all liquidation cases. The remaining three, which we look at in Chapter 10, govern the liquidation of special types of debtors, like stockbrokers.

Chapter 7 bankruptcy is bankruptcy in the old-fashioned sense. Filing a petition results in appointment of a trustee, who liquidates the estate and distributes the proceeds to creditors. The trustee is paid a commission on these distributions.[6]

The trustee acts on behalf of all the creditors, ensuring that the costs of pursuing a general liquidation are diminished and that creditors with small stakes can benefit from collection efforts that might have been too expensive to consider otherwise.

Upon commencement of the case, the court sends notice of the case to all creditors, along with notice of the meeting of creditors under section 341(a). If it appears that there are assets that will be distributed to creditors, the notice also informs creditors of the deadline for filing proofs of claim. Creditors are required to file proofs of their claims by a date specified by the court, usually ninety days after the initial meeting of creditors.

---

[3] Other permutations are discussed in Chapter 3 of THE LAW OF FAILURE, *supra* note 1.

[4] Bankruptcy Code § 727(a)(1).

[5] Under some state corporate statutes, a corporation that has completed a chapter 7 case may dissolve without complying with provisions that otherwise require the payment of (or reserve for) creditors.

[6] See Chapter 8 of this book for more on the chapter 7 trustee.

Creditors can form committees in chapter 7 cases, but all indications are that such committees are exceptionally rare.[7] One reason may be that, unlike their counterparts in chapter 11, chapter 7 committees have no ability to hire professionals paid by the estate.

Chapter 7 debtors can convert their cases to chapter 11, provided the debtor is eligible to be in chapter 11.[8] Perhaps more common is the debtor who starts in chapter 11 and then converts to chapter 7 once it becomes clear that a reorganization plan is impossible.[9] Creditors can also ask the court to convert a chapter 11 case to chapter 7, so a threatened conversion by either side may be part of the bargaining process in chapter 11.

As we will see, chapter 7 looms large in chapter 11, because much of the reorganization process is tested against the baseline of a hypothetical chapter 7. If a creditor or shareholder is not getting something more out of chapter 11 than they would get in chapter 7, they have no reason to participate in the far more complex and expensive process that is chapter 11. In short, chapter 7's "shadow effect" might be as important as, and perhaps even more important than, its direct effect.

SUMMARY

Chapter 7 has some similarities to a state corporate dissolution, but with enhanced abilities to recover assets for distribution to all creditors, and the benefits of the automatic stay. In theory, creditors could be actively engaged in a chapter 7 case, but since unsecured creditors rarely recover anything in chapter 7, participation is apt to be more theoretical than real.[10] Chapter 7's most significant role, at least from an economic perspective, is to provide a baseline for chapter 11. Chapter 7 also provides the endpoint for many failed chapter 11 cases.

---

[7]   Bankruptcy Code § 705.
[8]   Bankruptcy Code § 706(d).
[9]   Anne Lawton, *Chapter 11 Triage: Diagnosing A Debtor's Prospects for Success*, 54 ARIZ. L. REV. 985, 1011 (2012).
[10]   Stephen J. Lubben, *Business Liquidation*, 81 AM. BANKR. L.J. 65 (2007).

8. The chapter 7 trustee

Key concepts:

- The U.S. trustee
- The interim trustee
- Electing a trustee
- The trustee's duties in chapter 7

Every chapter 7 case has a trustee. Some may have several trustees during the life of the case.

Upon filing, an interim chapter 7 trustee is appointed by the United States Trustee, from a panel of trustees.[1] The interim trustee serves until the creditors elect a permanent trustee,[2] which sometimes never happens. In that case, the interim trustee becomes the permanent trustee.[3]

The United States Trustee Program is a unit of United States Department of Justice. U.S. Trustees are appointed for twenty-one regions across the country. Each U.S. Trustee is overseen by the program's main office in Washington D.C.

In general, the U.S. Trustee's primary role is to act as a "watchdog" in bankruptcy cases.[4] The U.S. Trustee also performs various administrative tasks in the bankruptcy system, including maintaining a pool of chapter 7 trustees – known as the "panel," and thus chapter 7 trustees are often referred to as panel trustees. Panel members must possess all of the qualifications established by the Attorney General of the United States, as well as the qualifications set forth in section 321 of the Bankruptcy Code.

---

[1] Bankruptcy Code § 701.
[2] Bankruptcy Code § 702.
[3] Bankruptcy Code § 702(d).
[4] For the duties of the U.S. Trustee, see 28 U.S.C. § 586.

The United States Trustee is distinct from the bankruptcy, panel, or chapter 7 trustee. But in some cases, the U.S. Trustee can act as the chapter 7 trustee, mostly when nobody else is willing or able to take on the appointment.[5]

As noted, it is unusual for creditors to elect a trustee in a chapter 7 case as permitted by section 702(c), and therefore the interim trustee becomes the permanent trustee in almost all chapter 7 cases. But in those rare chapter 7 cases where there are assets to be distributed, the creditors may want to elect a trustee to replace the interim or panel with a trustee more to their liking. Section 702 sets forth an elaborate process to do so.

All of the action happens at the "341 meeting," presided over by the interim trustee.[6] The meeting is required by section 341(a) of the Code, and provides an opportunity for the trustee and creditors to question the debtor (or the debtor's officer) under oath.[7]

It is at this meeting that creditors can request an election of a trustee. Section 702 seems to contemplate a vote on the issue of holding a trustee election – an election on holding an election? – since creditors holding at least 20 percent of claims must support the move before a trustee election will happen.[8] Creditors who are insiders or who have an interest materially adverse to the other unsecured creditors are barred from asking for an election, as the calculation is limited to creditors who may vote. Thus, a creditor who does not want to elect a new trustee can attempt to stop the election from even happening.[9]

Section 702 seems to assume that if an election is called, it will happen immediately after the decision to hold the election. But the presiding (interim) trustee may want to postpone the final vote until notice has been given to all creditors, especially if the decision to call the election was unexpected. Voting at the 341 meeting can also happen by proxy, but such proxies are subject to a mind-boggling

---

[5] Bankruptcy Code § 701(a)(2). Instances of the U.S. Trustee serving as bankruptcy trustee appear to be rare.

[6] The Code requires a meeting of creditors, under § 341(a). Under § 341(b), a meeting of shareholders could also be commenced, but by all accounts, these are rare, especially in chapter 7 cases.

[7] *See also* Bankruptcy Code § 343.

[8] A quorum consists of the same 20 percent of the total claims.

[9] And recall that the meeting will typically be presided over by the interim trustee, who may not want to be displaced as trustee.

complex set of regulations under the Federal Rules of Bankruptcy Procedure.[10]

Once a trustee is selected, one way or another, section 704 sets forth the trustee's duties in the case.[11] There are additional duties imposed by other sections of the Bankruptcy Code, such as with regard to depositing or investing money of the estate under section 345(a) or recovering from individual partners in a bankruptcy of the partnership case under section 723.

Most importantly, section 704 provides that the trustee shall, "collect and reduce to money the property of the estate for which such trustee serves, and close up such estate as expeditiously as is compatible with the best interests of parties in interest." Collecting the estate's assets may require the trustee to prosecute "turnover actions" under section 542, under which third parties holding the debtor's assets must deliver those assets to the trustee, or "avoidance actions," to recover preferences or fraudulent transfers (discussed in Chapter 6). In addition, the trustee may have to investigate not only the debtor, but perhaps also the debtor's principals.[12]

The failure of the trustee to carry out the duties set forth under section 704 may give rise to claims against the trustee by creditors. But absent extreme trustee misconduct, the trustee is protected against liability to bad-tempered creditors by a vaguely defined form of judicial immunity.[13]

As part of its general duty to maximize the value of the estate, the trustee may also request authority to operate the debtor's business.[14] This most often makes sense in a context where the trustee expects to sell the business as a going concern. But the fact that chapter 7 presumes that the trustee will not operate the debtor's

---

[10]   Bankruptcy Rule 2006. In the past, the election of bankruptcy trustees was the subject of several notorious bankruptcy scandals, and thus the Rules and § 702 seem designed to thwart that, perhaps at the cost of creating a process so complex that it is rarely used.

[11]   *See also* Bankruptcy Code §§ 321 to 325.

[12]   § 704(a)(4) expressly provides that the trustee shall "investigate the financial affairs of the debtor." Often that investigation will lead the trustee to have to investigate those with control over the debtor as well.

[13]   In re J & S Properties, LLC, 872 F.3d 138, 143 (3d Cir. 2017).

[14]   Bankruptcy Code § 721.

business provides an important point of distinction with chapter 11, as we will soon see.

SUMMARY

The chapter 7 trustee assigned on the day the case is filed will normally come from the panel of trustees standing ready for such cases. In many instances, that interim trustee will remain in place throughout the case. But in cases involving sizable assets, including cases converted from chapter 11, the creditors might consider it worthwhile to appoint a different trustee. Whoever is appointed will play the key role in gathering the debtor's assets and selling the same for the benefits of the creditors.

9. Distributing the chapter 7 estate

> **Key concepts:**
>
> - Abandonment
> - Priorities in liquidation
> - Paying the trustee

We return to a topic we touched on in Chapter 4, the payment of the estate proceeds to creditors. As we noted in the prior Chapter, one of the trustee's key duties is to liquidate the estate's assets and distribute the proceeds to creditors.[1] The Code provides clear guidance for the final distribution of the estate, but there are several ways that creditors, particularly secured creditors, may receive a distribution earlier than other creditors.

The trustee may seek authorization to "abandon" property of the estate that is "burdensome to the estate or of inconsequential value to the estate." Alternatively, a creditor can request that the court order the trustee to abandon property.[2] In either case, the abandonment requires court approval. Although the Code does not say so explicitly, abandoned property reverts to the debtor, unless the court orders otherwise.

A trustee will frequently abandon property when liens on the property exceed its value. That is, when there is nothing left that will benefit the estate, the property is of "inconsequential value" to the estate.[3] Following abandonment, secured creditors will be able to enforce their rights against the property.

---

[1]   *See* Bankruptcy Code § 704(a)(1); § 726, discussed later in this Chapter, dictates the order of distribution for the funds.

[2]   Bankruptcy Code § 554.

[3]   Sometimes the trustee will get it wrong. In In re Charles Frederick Biehl, Ch. 7 Case No. 6:13-bk-26277-MH (Bankr. C.D. Cal. Jan. 16, 2018) (docket 233), the Bankruptcy Court rejected a trustee's request to revoke abandonment of real

But the Supreme Court, in a case called *Midlantic National Bank v. New Jersey Department of Environmental Protection*,[4] developed an environmental hazard exception to the abandonment power, which prevents trustees from abandoning property that represents an environmental hazard. This is consistent with federal environmental laws that seek to keep all present and future owners of property "on the hook" for environmental cleanup costs.[5]

Property in the estate that the trustee does not sell is automatically abandoned at the close of the bankruptcy case.[6] If the property has any value, it will represent a source of creditor recovery outside the bankruptcy process.[7] Regardless of value, it will be one of the few assets a business debtor owns once the chapter 7 process is complete.[8]

Section 725, which allows the trustee to make an early distribution of property in which another party holds an interest, works in tandem with section 554. The actual amount of property distributed under section 725 is likely small, since in many cases property of

---

property when the trustee received an offer to purchase the property more than one year after the abandonment became effective.

[4]   474 U.S. 494, 506 (1986).

[5]   Later courts have diverged on whether the Supreme Court's holding is limited to just those instances where the environmental contamination represents a serious public health hazard. Footnote nine of the Court's opinion typically is cited in support of such a limited reading of the case. In that footnote, Justice Powell, writing for the majority, explained that:

> This exception to the abandonment power vested in the trustee by § 554 is a narrow one. It does not encompass a speculative or indeterminate future violation of such laws that may stem from abandonment. The abandonment power is not to be fettered by laws or regulations not reasonably calculated to protect the public health or safety from imminent and identifiable harm.

474 U.S. at 507 n.9.

[6]   Bankruptcy Code § 554(c). The rule only applies to property that was disclosed on the debtor's schedules of assets and liabilities, required by § 521. If the property was not scheduled, § 554(d) applies, and it is not abandoned.

[7]   During the pendency of the case, creditors will typically seek to lift the automatic stay under § 362(d) before pursuing such property. Although the stay under § 362(a)(3) and (4) which protects the *estate's interest* in the property, is automatically terminated by abandonment because the property is no longer property of the estate, provisions of § 362(a) protecting the *debtor's interest* may not be terminated by abandonment.

[8]   This is probably fairly theoretical. If the trustee does not want the asset, it seems unlikely that creditors will rush to grab it.

this kind will have been previously sold under section 363,[9] abandoned under section 554, or foreclosed upon by a secured creditor after the stay was lifted under section 362(d). But property that was in the debtor's possession on the petition day as part of a consignment or bailment might go back to its original owner under section 725.[10]

The trustee must file a notice of her intent to use section 725. As with most motion practice under the Code, a hearing will only be held if somebody objects. In a business chapter 7 case, where the debtor is apt to be somewhat passive, especially if its officers have long gone, there might be few to object to the trustee's plans.

Section 726 is the heart of chapter 7 distribution scheme. That section creates a "waterfall" – six layers of unsecured claims to be paid in the order they are listed. Secured creditors are assumed to have received the value of their collateral outside this process, perhaps under either sections 554 or 725.[11]

First comes priority claims, as defined in section 507, including administrative claims.[12] Note that if the chapter 7 case was originally filed under chapter 11, and then converted to chapter 7, under section 726(b), priority claims from the earlier chapter 11 case are subordinated to the priority claims of the chapter 7 case. That is, the costs of running the chapter 7 case come before the unpaid costs of running the (failed) chapter 11 case.

Following priority claims, property of the estate is distributed next under Code section 726(a) to general unsecured creditors. Creditors who filed timely claims come before creditors who filed late claims.[13] Certainly penalties are pushed to the back of the line. Once they are fully paid, then unsecured creditors are entitled to interest.[14]

---

[9]   *See* Chapter 16, *infra*, for more on § 363.
[10]   Provided the trustee cannot avoid the consignment or bailment under its "strong arm" powers, as discussed in Chapter 6.
[11]   The payment of secured creditors is never clearly explained in the Code, and instead the drafters seem to have treated it as one of those things that "everybody knows."
[12]   *See* Chapter 4 for a further discussion.
[13]   Bankruptcy Code §§ 726(a)(2), (a)(3).
[14]   As we discussed in Chapter 4, the bankruptcy petition stops the accrual of interest on unsecured claims, but not on secured claims with available collateral.

Only if there is any money left after making all those distributions will the trustee turn to the debtor.[15] In such an unlikely event, the debtor would presumably pay the proceeds as a shareholder dividend upon dissolution under state law.

SUMMARY

Once the trustee has reduced all of the debtor's assets to cash, she can distribute those assets under the payment "waterfall" set forth in section 726. But even before that distribution begins, the trustee may have abandoned property under section 554 or otherwise distributed under section 725 to somebody else with an ownership interest in the property.

---

[15]   Bankruptcy Code § 726(a)(6).

10. Special chapter 7 cases

Key concepts:

- Securities brokers' bankruptcy
- SIPA
- Commodities brokers' bankruptcy
- CFTC and SEC receiverships
- Clearing banks in bankruptcy

For most bankruptcy attorneys, chapter 7 begins and ends with subchapters I and II. But in certain special cases – those involving securities brokers, commodities brokers, and some "clearing banks" – additional subchapters of chapter 7 apply. This Chapter provides a brief overview of these parts of chapter 7, while also noting the other insolvency systems that are open to those debtors.

Because stock and commodity brokers are not allowed in chapter 11, a threshold issue in many of the small number of reported cases under the special subchapters of chapter 7 involve definitional questions. Namely, if the debtor is property classified as a stock or commodities broker, its chapter 11 case cannot proceed. Even within chapter 7, the question of whether a debtor is a stock or commodity broker can have import, since distributions are made under a different set of priorities.[1]

Subchapter III of the Bankruptcy Code applies to stockbrokers, but only those stockbrokers that are not members of Securities Investor Protection Corporation ("SIPC"). SIPC registered brokers are instead liquidated under the Securities Investor Protection Act ("SIPA").[2] SIPA borrows large parts of the Bankruptcy Code to fill in its content, and cases under the statute are typically heard by

---

[1]   In re Baker & Getty Fin. Servs., 106 F.3d 1255, 1260 (6th Cir. 1997).
[2]   15 U.S.C. §§ 78aaa–78lll.

bankruptcy judges, but it is a liquidation process distinct from chapter 7.[3]

Since all businesses or individuals registered as brokers or dealers under section 15(b) of the Securities and Exchange Act of 1934 must be members of SIPC, chapter 7, subchapter III is a backstop for the more broadly applicable stockbroker insolvency mechanism in SIPA.[4] Subchapter III is most often invoked in the case of small, intrastate brokers (not registered under the '34 Act) and in cases involving (illegal) unlicensed brokers, who were not members of SIPC. Those sorts of cases do not arise too often.

Brokers must segregate customer property from debtor property, and that fund of customer property is used to pay customer claims first. Both SIPA and chapter 7 involve the appointment of a trustee, who liquidates the estate for the primary benefit of customers.[5] In a SIPA case, customers also benefit from SIPC insurance which fills any gaps in the customer property fund, up to $500,000 per customer (with a sublimit of $250,000 for cash in brokerage accounts).[6] In chapter 7, there is no insurance fund to fill in gaps, but the process otherwise works the same, with the customers getting first shot at the customer fund.

Customers of commodity brokers also benefit from a priority claim against a broker's fund of customer property, but there is no insurance system to backstop the segregation of funds here.[7] For that reason, commodity broker liquidations under subchapter IV of chapter 7 more closely resemble those of non-SIPC broker-dealers under subchapter III.[8]

---

[3] 15 U.S.C. § 78fff(b). *See* 15 U.S.C. § 78fff-1(b).

[4] Bankruptcy Code § 742 provides that the filing of a protective decree under SIPA stays all proceedings under the Code unless and until such application is dismissed.

[5] In a SIPA case the trustee is choose by SIPC and confirmed by the bankruptcy court, while in chapter 7 the court appoints the trustee directly.

[6] SIPC, in addition to advancing sufficient funds required by SIPA for customer claims under 15 U.S.C. § 78fff-3(a), advances funds to the trustee to pay costs and expenses of administration of the estate, to the extent that the estate is insufficient. 15 U.S.C. § 78fff-3(b).

[7] Bankruptcy Code § 766(h); In re Bucyrus Grain Co., Inc., 127 B.R. 45, 48 (D. Kan. 1988).

[8] Although the CFTC has no authority to commence a case, Code § 762 requires the clerk of the bankruptcy court to give the CFTC prompt notice of a petition. The title of subchapter IV is a bit misleading, because a close look at the

The Commodity Futures Trading Commission ("CFTC") – the primary regulator of commodity brokers, or futures commission merchants ("FCMs"), as they are often called in CFTC speak – has authority to write rules for broker insolvencies.[9] Cases under subchapter IV thus involve a mixture of both the Code and CFTC regulations.[10] In cases where the debtor was both a SIPC member stock broker and a commodities broker, the case can proceed under SIPA, but SIPC insurance still does not extend to commodities customers.

The final, and most obscure, special subchapter of chapter 7 is subchapter V. It has never been used.

Banks are normally entirely outside of the Bankruptcy Code, but under subchapter V some "clearing banks" are permitted to seek relief under chapter 7, if the Federal Reserve allows it. The same banks can file chapter 11 cases without any input from the Fed.

Untangling Bankruptcy Code section 109 a bit, we can see that these special clearing banks come in two forms, those who are uninsured state member banks, and those who are Edge Act companies (those companies organized under section 25A of the Federal Reserve Act). Not all Edge Act companies, or uninsured state member banks, may file under chapter 7 – only those who are also engaged in clearing. Thus it appears that subchapter V applies to two financial institutions, and perhaps nobody else: Depository Trust Company, a subsidiary of The Depository Trust & Clearing Corporation, and the CLS Bank.

The first provides securities depository, clearing, and settlement services for more than 1.3 million traded securities issues valued at $54.2 trillion (as of 2017), including securities issued in the US and more than 131 countries and territories. The second, CLS Bank, provides foreign exchange settlement services to banks, brokers,

---

definition of "commodity broker" reveals that it covers all sorts of brokers and clearing organizations for a broad array of derivatives, not just those involving corn, wheat, or frozen orange juice concentrate.

[9]   7 U.S.C. § 24.

[10]   *See* 17 C.F.R. § 190.01-.10 & appendices. § 190.08(a)(1)(ii)(J) provides that, "only to the extent that" the enumerated types of customer property are insufficient to satisfy in full all claims of public customers, other estate property will be used to satisfy those claims. The bankruptcy court in In re Griffin Trading Co., 245 B.R. 291 (Bankr. N.D. Ill. 2000), found that this provision exceeded the CFTC's authority.

funds, and corporations. It handles more than $5 trillion of such foreign exchange trades each *day*.

Both are giants in their realms, and one suspects that chapter 7 cases involving either would not be pretty. Subchapter V sets forth additional powers of a chapter 7 trustee in a clearing bank liquidation, including the ability to transfer the assets of the clearing bank to a "bridge bank" as the FDIC can do with regard to a failed insured bank or under Dodd-Frank's OLA.[11] That provides some indication of what the plan might be in any case filed thereunder. But it seems more likely that either entity would be resolved under some other process – maybe even a receivership. Why subchapter V was enacted is unclear.

SUMMARY

Three subchapters of chapter 7 provide special liquidation procedures for debtors in regulated industries. For both stock and commodity brokers, these special subchapters are the only way in which these debtors can file a case under the Bankruptcy Code.[12] Subchapter V applies to perhaps only two entities, but these entities can also file under chapter 11 (and the Federal Reserve also has some ability to place either into a receivership).

---

[11]   Bankruptcy Code § 783.
[12]   In many cases, the SEC and the CFTC have used federal court receiverships to liquidate stock and commodities brokers, particularly in cases involving fraud.

PART IV

Reorganization under chapter 11

11. An introduction to chapter 11 of the Bankruptcy Code

Key concepts:

- Reorganization and liquidation under chapter 11
- The debtor in possession or DIP
- Examiners
- Chapter 11 trustees

So at last we make it to chapter 11. At a high level of generality, chapter 11 is simple: the debtor, acting as trustee, negotiates a reorganization plan with its stakeholders. But within that broad framework, chapter 11 facilitates a wide range of potential corporate reorganizations.

Although chapter 11 is often associated with the reorganization of a company as a going concern, it also provides a framework for the orderly liquidation of a company. Indeed, it is widely believed to be better at that task than chapter 7, at least for large firms. Typically such a liquidation is achieved by adoption of a "liquidating plan."[1] That is, just as there can be reorganization plans, there can be plans that provide for the sale of the debtor's assets and the distribution of the proceeds under the terms of the plan.

Sometimes the liquidation plan is preceded by an asset sale – often termed a "363 sale," for the section of the Code that authorizes them. We return to 363 sales in Chapter 16, but the basic idea is that the debtor can sell its assets before negotiating a plan to distribute the proceeds.[2]

---

[1] Bankruptcy Code § 1123(a)(5)(D).
[2] Creditors who do not like how those negotiations are going might move to convert the case to chapter 7.

Under chapter 11, the presumption is that the debtor will continue to conduct business as usual,[3] and that there will be no trustee. Instead, the debtor acts as the trustee, with the title of "debtor in possession" or "DIP." The DIP is the debtor – in possession of its own bankruptcy estate, and with duties that largely track those of a chapter 7 trustee.[4]

Whenever the Code says trustee, we can read in "debtor in possession" (or "DIP").[5] For example, in a chapter 11 case, we can read section 365(a) as follows:

> Except as provided in sections 765 and 766 of this title and in subsections (b), (c), and (d) of this section, the [DIP], subject to the court's approval, may assume or reject any executory contract or unexpired lease of the debtor.

This introduces one of the stranger aspects of chapter 11 bankruptcy: the debtor acting as DIP suddenly has the power to undo actions taken by the pre-bankruptcy debtor, even though the same people may be acting as the debtor's officers or directors. This strangeness reaches its height with regard to the avoidance powers,[6] where the DIP (acting through its management) might seek to undo a payment or transfer that the same management made just before bankruptcy. The key difference is that the DIP now acts as a trustee, with a fiduciary duty to the bankruptcy estate.[7]

Sections 363(b) and (c) authorize the DIP to act in "the ordinary course of business." The DIP can take extraordinary action, but only with court approval (although the court typically defers to the

---

[3] Bankruptcy Code § 1108 ("Unless the court, on request of a party in interest and after notice and a hearing, orders otherwise, the trustee may operate the debtor's business."). As discussed in the text, and footnote 5, by reading §§ 1101(1) and 1107(a), we can see that § 1108 empowers the debtor to continue to operate its own business. Recall that a trustee can operate the business in chapter 7, but only with court approval. Bankruptcy Code § 704(8). Chapter 11 thus flips the presumption.

[4] Bankruptcy Code §§ 1106(a), 1107(a).

[5] Under § 1101 of the Bankruptcy Code, we learn that "debtor in possession" normally means the debtor, and then under § 1107(a) the debtor in possession is given the powers of a trustee.

[6] Refer to Chapter 6.

[7] *See generally* Martin J. Bienenstock, *Conflicts Between Management and the Debtor in Possession's Fiduciary Duties*, 61 U. CIN. L. REV. 543 (1992).

debtor's "business judgment" on most matters, especially in the absence of objection from creditors or other stakeholders).

Formal bankruptcy trustees can be appointed in chapter 11 cases, but they are the exception rather than the rule.[8] Even in cases of massive fraud – Enron, for example – trustees are rarely appointed. Instead, new management may take control, often before or just after the bankruptcy filing.

Instead of a trustee, the court may appoint an "examiner" to investigate the pre-bankruptcy conduct of the debtor, or its insiders, without ousting the debtor from possession.[9] Examiners were appointed in the Enron and Lehman Brothers cases, to prepare reports about "what happened." Often such reports are key to facilitating a plan: only with agreement on the background facts can the parties "move on" to discuss how to divide up the estate. But examiners are not free; their fees and the fees of their professionals add to the cost of the chapter 11 process.[10]

A bankruptcy court must convert or dismiss a chapter 11 case if a party in interest establishes "cause," unless unusual circumstances specifically identified by the court dictate otherwise.[11] The debtor has a unilateral right to convert to chapter 7, which sometimes can be usefully used as a threat to corral holdout creditors.[12]

Subchapter I of chapter 11 (sections 1101–1114) deals with special parties and roles found only in chapter 11 – like examiners and creditors committees.[13] Subchapters II and III (sections 1121–1146) deal with plan formulation and confirmation.

And subchapter IV (sections 1161–1174) provides special provisions dealing only with railroads. Railroad reorganization is a specialized area of practice; recall that railroads are not allowed in chapter 7 at all.[14] Among other things, railroad cases reverse the

---

[8] Bankruptcy Code § 1104(a)(1).

[9] Bankruptcy Code § 1104(b).

[10] We come back to the issue of cost in Chapter 13, which covers the retention of professionals. The cost of examiners includes both the cost of the examiner herself, and the cost of professionals retained by the examiner.

[11] Bankruptcy Code § 1112(b)(1).

[12] Bankruptcy Code § 1112(a). *But cf.* Marrama v. Citizens Bank of Massachusetts, 549 U.S. 365, 374 (2007) (individual debtor's right to convert from chapter 7 to chapter 13 can be lost when debtor acts in bad faith).

[13] On the latter, see Chapter 13.

[14] *See* Chapter 2.

normal rule of chapter 11, and a trustee is appointed in every case. In addition, liquidation of a railroad debtor is strictly constrained. When the Bankruptcy Code was adopted in 1978 railroads were still heavily regulated by the Interstate Commerce Commission, which was eventually abolished in 1995.[15]

In its more traditional incarnation, the chapter 11 process is predicated on the belief that allowing the debtor to continue normal operations, under its existing management, will result in gains for all stakeholders. In particular, chapter 11 aims to capture the difference between the value of company as a going concern, and its value if liquidated in a traditional bankruptcy case under chapter 7. Courts often give another reason, either explicitly or implicitly, for using chapter 11 in place of chapter 7 – there is value in preserving business operations, to employees, the community, the economy generally, so it is worth trying to keep operating, despite the debtor's insolvency, if possible.

Overall, bankruptcy under chapter 11 is best seen as a corporate transaction, supervised by the court, rather than an exclusively judicial process.[16] It is both court case and transaction, simultaneously.

SUMMARY

Chapter 11 may be a useful tool to reorganize, or gradually liquidate, a large business.[17] The debtor (and the debtor's management) take on the role of trustee, avoiding the disruption that often comes in chapter 7 from replacement of management with a randomly selected trustee. The court may appoint a trustee in a chapter 11 case, but more often prior bad acts will be the subject of an investigation by an independent examiner. And to the greatest

---

[15] Railroads are currently regulated, to a lesser degree, by the U.S. Surface Transportation Board and the Federal Railroad Administration. The latter is part of the United States Department of Transportation.

[16] Melissa B. Jacoby, *What Should Judges Do in Chapter 11?*, 2015 U. ILL. L. REV. 571 (2015).

[17] *Cf.* Mission Prod. Holdings, Inc. v. Tempnology, LLC, No. 17-1657, 2019 WL 2166392, at *8 (U.S. May 20, 2019) ("The Code of course aims to make reorganizations possible. But it does not permit anything and everything that might advance that goal.").

extent possible under the circumstances, the debtor attempts to keep on doing what it does, as if nothing has happened.

12. Stabilizing the debtor's business in chapter 11

> **Key concepts:**
>
> - First-day motions and orders
> - Utility companies under the Code
> - DIP financing
> - Use of cash collateral

As a matter of grand theory, when a debtor files a chapter 11 case, it pays its routine post-bankruptcy debts in the ordinary course,[1] its non-routine obligations with court permission,[2] and all of its pre-bankruptcy debts are dealt with under the plan.[3] That works fine as a matter of theory, but for an operating company – as most chapter 11 debtors are – it is often not super clear which debts are pre- and post-bankruptcy.

And while the Code – and the Federal Rules of Bankruptcy Procedure and the United States Trustee's office – set forth many rules to delineate the line between the pre-bankruptcy debtor and the DIP, often it will not reflect good business sense to follow these rules.[4]

As a result of these and other considerations, it has become common practice to file, together with the chapter 11 petition, a package of "first-day" motions. Some first-day motions address

---

[1]   Bankruptcy Code § 363(c); *see also* Bankruptcy Code § 1108.
[2]   Bankruptcy Code § 363(b).
[3]   And these creditors are precluded from enforcing during the case by the automatic stay in § 363.
[4]   A good example is the U.S. Trustee's rule that requires DIPs to set up all new bank accounts. A large corporation typically has a complicated cash management system, and it makes little sense to recreate that upon a bankruptcy filing.

administrative matters, or retention of professionals in the case.[5] But a large number of the first-day motions seek immediate court orders allowing the debtor to deviate from the strict terms of the Code and related rules and regulations. The justification for all such motions is, at heart, that full compliance with the Code would undermine the broader goals of chapter 11.

The first-day motions are typically considered by the court at an emergency hearing, very early in the case (as the name suggests, sometimes on the first day of the case). An agenda for such a "first day" hearing is shown in Figure 12.1 below. In his declaration in support of these first-day motions, this debtor's CFO wrote that

> The Debtors have filed a number of First Day Motions seeking relief necessary to stabilize their business operations, facilitate the efficient administration of these chapter 11 cases, and protect the value of their estates. The relief requested in each of the First Day Motions is critical to maximize the value of these estates. I believe the relief requested in the First Day Motions is essential to allow the Debtors to operate with minimal disruption during the pendency of these chapter 11 cases.

This paragraph could be taken from almost any first-day declaration – all CFOs will say something like this in support of the first-day motions.

Typically, the chapter 11 debtor will file first-day motions like the following:

- A motion for authorization to pay certain pre-bankruptcy claims, including employee claims and claims of "critical vendors."
- A motion for certain administrative orders that, *e.g.*, set regular hearing dates, consolidate (for administrative purposes) the cases of related debtors, and establish a procedure for the payment of the debtor's professionals.
- A motion to assure that the debtor's utility service will remain in place.
- A motion to approve "debtor-in-possession" financing negotiated by the debtor and its lenders, or to approve, under specified conditions, the debtor's use of "cash collateral."

---

[5] We circle back to professional retention in Chapter 14.

Edward O. Sassower, P.C.
Joshua A. Sussberg, P.C. (*pro hac vice* admission pending)
KIRKLAND & ELLIS LLP
KIRKLAND & ELLIS INTERNATIONAL LLP
601 Lexington Avenue
New York, New York 10022
Telephone: (212) 446-4800
Facsimile: (212) 446-4900

-and-

Michael A. Condyles (VA 27807)
Peter J. Barrett (VA 46179)
Jeremy S. Williams (VA 77469)
KUTAK ROCK LLP
901 East Byrd Street, Suite 1000
Richmond, Virginia 23219-4071
Telephone: (804) 644-1700
Facsimile: (804) 783-6192

James H.M. Sprayregen, P.C.
Anup Sathy, P.C.
Chad J. Husnick, P.C. (*pro hac vice* admission pending)
Robert A. Britton (*pro hac vice* admission pending)
Emily E. Geier (*pro hac vice* admission pending)
KIRKLAND & ELLIS LLP
KIRKLAND & ELLIS INTERNATIONAL LLP
300 North LaSalle
Chicago, Illinois 60654
Telephone: (312) 862-2000
Facsimile: (312) 862-2200

Proposed Co-Counsel to the Debtors and Debtors in Possession

IN THE UNITED STATES BANKRUPTCY COURT
FOR THE EASTERN DISTRICT OF VIRGINIA
RICHMOND DIVISION

In re:	)	Chapter 11
	)	
TOYS "R" US, INC., *et al.*,[1]	)	Case No. 17-34665 (KLP)
	)	
Debtors.	)	(Joint Administration Requested)
	)	

FIRST DAY AGENDA FOR HEARING ON
SEPTEMBER 19, 2017, AT 11:00 A.M. (PREVAILING EASTERN TIME)

I.   INTRODUCTION[2]:

1.   Declaration of David A. Brandon, Chairman of the Board and Chief Executive Officer of Toys "R" Us, Inc., in Support of Chapter 11 Petitions and First Day Motions [Docket No. 20].

---

[1]   The Debtors in these chapter 11 cases, along with the last four digits of each Debtor's federal tax identification number, are set forth in the *Debtors' Motion for Entry of an Order (I) Directing Joint Administration of Chapter 11 Cases and (II) Granting Related Relief* filed contemporaneously herewith. The location of the Debtors' service address is One Geoffrey Way, Wayne, NJ 07470.

[2]   In support of the motions set forth herein and the relief requested in connection with the "First Day Motions", the Debtors have submitted the *Declaration of David A. Brandon, Chairman of the Board and Chief Executive Officer of Toys "R" Us, Inc., In Support of Chapter 11 Petitions and First Day Motions* and *Declaration of Michael J. Short, Chief Financial Officer of Toys "R" Us, Inc., In Support of Debtors' First Day Motions* [Docket Nos. 20, 30].

2. Declaration of Michael J. Short, Chief Financial Officer of Toys "R" Us, Inc., in Support of Debtors' First Day Motions [Docket No. 30].

3. "Motion to Expedite First Day Hearing" *Debtors' Motion for an Expedited Hearing on "First Day Motions"* [Docket No. 35].

4. "Pro Hac Vice" *Motions of Certain Attorneys from Kirkland & Ellis LLP Pursuant to Local Bankruptcy Rule 2090-1(E)(2) for Admission Pro Hac Vice* [Docket Nos. 23-27].

5. "Joint Administration Motion" *Debtors' Motion for Entry of an Order (I) Directing Joint Administration of Chapter 11 Cases and (II) Granting Related Relief* [Docket No. 10].

II. FINANCING

6. "DIP & Cash Collateral Motion (Domestic)" *Debtors' Motion for Entry of Interim and Final Orders (I) Authorizing the North American Debtors to Obtain Postpetition Financing, (II) Authorizing the North American Debtors to Use Cash Collateral, (III) Granting Liens and Providing Superpriority Administrative Expense Status, (IV) Granting Adequate Protection to the Prepetition Lenders, (V) Modifying the Automatic Stay, (VI) Scheduling A Final Hearing, and (VII) Granting Related Relief* [Docket No. 29].

7. "DIP & Cash Collateral Motion (International)" *Debtors' Motion for Entry of Interim and Final Orders (I) Authorizing the TRU Taj Debtors to Obtain Postpetition Financing, (II) Authorizing the TRU Taj Debtors to Use Cash Collateral, (III) Granting Liens and Providing Superpriority Administrative Expense Status, (IV) Granting Adequate Protection to the Prepetition Lenders, (V) Modifying the Automatic Stay, (VI) Scheduling A Final Hearing, and (VII) Granting Related Relief* [Docket No. 32].

    A. *Declaration of David Kurtz in Support of the Debtors' Motions for Entry of Interim and Final Orders (I) Authorizing the Debtors to Obtain North American and International Postpetition Financing, (II) Authorizing the Debtors to Use Cash Collateral, (III) Granting Liens and Providing Superpriority Administrative Expense Status, (IV) Granting Adequate Protection to the Prepetition Lenders, (V) Modifying the Automatic Stay, (VI) Scheduling A Final Hearing, and (VII) Granting Related Relief* [Docket No. 33].

III. OPERATIONAL MOTIONS

8.   "Cash Management Motion" *Debtors' Motion for Entry of Interim and Final Orders (I) Authorizing the Debtors to (A) Continue to Operate Their Cash Management System, (B) Honor Certain Prepetition Obligations Related Thereto, (C) Maintain Existing Business Forms, and (D) Perform Intercompany Transactions, and (II) Granting Related Relief* [Docket No. 22].

9.   "Wages Motion" *Debtors' Motion for Entry of Interim and Final Orders (I) Authorizing the Debtors to (A) Pay Prepetition Wages, Salaries, Other Compensation, and Reimbursable Expenses and (B) Continue Employee Benefits Programs, and (II) Granting Related Relief* [Docket No. 21].

10. "Lienholders Motion" *Debtors' Motion for Entry of Interim and Final Orders (I) Authorizing the Debtors to Pay Prepetition Claims of Lien Claimants, Import Claimants, and 503 (B) (9) Claimants, (II) Confirming Administrative Expense Priority of Outstanding Orders, and (III) Granting Related Relief* [Docket No. 14].

11. "Customer Programs Motion" *Debtors' Motion for Entry of Interim and Final Orders (I) Authorizing the Debtors to Pay Certain Prepetition Claims of Critical Vendors and (II) Granting Related Relief* [Docket No. 15].

12. "Taxes Motion" *Debtors' Motion for Entry of Interim and Final Orders (I) Authorizing the Payment of Certain Prepetition and Postpetition Taxes and Fees and (II) Granting Related Relief* [Docket No. 12].

13. "NOL Motion" *Debtors' Motion for Entry of Interim and Final Orders (I) Approving Notification and Hearing Procedures for Certain Transfers of and Declarations of Worthlessness with Respect to Common Stock, and (II) Granting Related Relief* [Docket No. 13].

14. "Critical Vendors Motion" *Debtors' Motion for Entry of Interim and Final Orders (I) Authorizing the Debtors to Pay Certain Prepetition Claims of Critical Vendors and (II) Granting Related Relief* [Docket No. 6].

15. "Foreign Vendors Motion" *Debtors' Motion for Entry of Interim and Final Orders (I) Authorizing the Debtors to Pay Prepetition Claims of Foreign Vendors; and (II) Granting Related Relief* [Docket No. 5].

16. "Insurance Motion" *Debtors' Motion for Entry of Interim and Final Orders (I) Authorizing the Debtors to (A) Continue and Renew Their Liability, Property, Casualty, and Other Insurance Policies and Honor All Obligations in Respect Thereof, and (B) Continue the Surety Bond Programs, and (II) Granting Related Relief* [Docket No. 16].

17. "Utilities Motion" *Debtors' Motion for Entry of Interim and Final Orders (I) Approving the Debtors' Proposed Adequate Assurance of Payment for Future*

Utility Services, (II) Prohibiting Utility Companies from Altering, Refusing, or Discontinuing Services, (III) Approving the Debtors' Proposed Procedures for Resolving Additional Assurance Requests, and (IV) Granting Related Relief [Docket No. 11].

IV.   ADMINISTRATIVE MOTIONS

18.   "Cross-Border Insolvency Protocol" *Debtors' Motion for Entry of Interim and Final Orders (I) Authorizing the Debtors to Pay Certain Prepetition Claims of Critical Vendors and (II) Granting Related Relief* [Docket No. 7].

19.   "Case Management Procedures Motion" *Debtors' Motion for Entry of an Order (I) Establishing Certain Notice, Case Management, and Administrative Procedures and (II) Granting Related Relief* [Docket No. 9].

20.   "Notice of Commencement" *Debtors' Motion for Entry of an Order Approving the Form and Manner of Notice of Commencement of the Chapter 11 Cases* [Docket No. 28].

21.   "Creditor Matrix, SOFAs, and Schedules Motion" *Debtors' Motion for Entry of an Order (I) Extending Time to File Schedules and Statements of Financial Affairs, (II) Authorizing the Debtors to File a Consolidated List of Creditors in Lieu of Submitting a Mailing Matrix for Each Debtor, (III) Authorizing the Debtors to File a Consolidated List of the Debtors' 50 Largest Unsecured Creditors, and (IV) Granting Related Relief* [Docket No. 3].

V.   RETENTION APPLICATIONS:

22.   "Claims and Noticing Agent Retention Application" *Debtors' Application for Entry of an Order (I) Authorizing the Debtors to Employ and Retain Prime Clerk LLC as Claims and Noticing Agent, Effective* Nunc Pro Tunc *to the Petition Date and (II) Granting Related Relief* [Docket No. 4].

[*Remainder of page intentionally left blank*]

Richmond, Virginia
Dated: September 19, 2017

/s/ *Michael A. Condyles*
KUTAK ROCK LLP
Michael A. Condyles (VA 27807)
Peter J. Barrett (VA 46179)
Jeremy S. Williams (VA 77469)
901 East Byrd Street, Suite 1000
Richmond, Virginia 23219-4071
Telephone: (804) 644-1700
Facsimile: (804) 783-6192
Email: Michael.Condyles@KutakRock.com
          Peter.Barrett@KutakRock.com
          Jeremy.Williams@KutakRock.com

*Proposed Co-Counsel to the Debtors
and Debtors in Possession*

KIRKLAND & ELLIS LLP
KIRKLAND & ELLIS INTERNATIONAL LLP
Edward O. Sassower, P.C.
Joshua A. Sussberg, P.C.
(*pro hac vice* admission pending)
601 Lexington Avenue
New York, New York 10022
Telephone: (212) 446-4800
Facsimile: (212) 446-4900
Email: edward.sassower@kirkland.com
          joshua.sussberg@kirkland.com

-and-

James H.M. Sprayregen, P.C.
Anup Sathy, P.C.
Chad J. Husnick, P.C.
(*pro hac vice* admission pending)
Robert A. Britton (*pro hac vice* admission pending)
Emily E. Geier (*pro hac vice* admission pending)
300 North LaSalle
Chicago, Illinois 60654
Telephone: (312) 862-2000
Facsimile: (312) 862-2200
Email: james.sprayregen@kirkland.com
          anup.sathy@kirkland.com
          chad.husnick@kirkland.com
          robert.britton@kirkland.com
          emily.geier@kirkland.com

*Proposed Co-Counsel to the Debtors
and Debtors in Possession*

KE 49373990

Figure 12.1

PRE-BANKRUPTCY CLAIMS

As suggested earlier, one or more first-day motions will seek authorization to pay certain pre-petition creditors in full right away. Typically included in this group are employees, whose first paycheck after the filing date will inevitably include pay for work done before the filing. If they are told they will have to wait for that portion of their pay until the end of the case, they may decide to stop showing up for work.[6]

Other similar motions may include unpaid, foreign creditors, who may be practically immune from the automatic stay and thus the bankruptcy process, and various "critical" trade vendors. This last category may be subject to abuse, but the basic idea is that some trade creditors might be so irritated at not getting paid that they will stop doing business with the debtor post-petition.

For example, a railroad that delivers the waterproof canvas to Bogartco's trenchcoat factory might be owed payment for a delivery right before bankruptcy. The automatic stay prevents it from suing to collect on that debt, but it can decline take new orders from Bogartco after bankruptcy.[7] Failure to receive shipments could have serious implications for the debtor's ongoing business, so, Bogartco will argue, it is in everyone's interest to pay the railroad and keep them happy.

A similar argument might be made with regard to the canvas vendor. Bogartco might be able to find a new canvas vendor, but changing a key vendor could cause significant disruption. Arguably, in the early days of the case, it's worth paying the current vendor's pre-petition claim to avoid that disruption.

Nothing in chapter 11, or the Bankruptcy Code generally, allows the payment of pre-petition employee or creditor debt other than under the plan. Debtors and their counsel typically rely on one of two arguments to support these sorts of motions. The first draws on two ancient equitable doctrines from nineteenth century railroad

---

[6]   Having a priority claim under section 507 quite understandably is not sufficient for most employees.

[7]   The result might be different if the railroad had a long-term contract with the debtor. Here I am assuming the railroad is paid for each delivery individually.

receiverships.[8] Of course, the extension of railroad doctrines, from an age when railroads were treated as vital public utilities, to companies generally, involves something of a logical leap. Most debtors' attorneys will ignore that leap if judges let them.

The other line of argument involves section 363, which allows the debtor to use its property in the ordinary course of business and, with court permission, even in non-ordinary situations. The argument here is that the debtor can use its property with court permission, perhaps upon a finding that doing so will benefit the estate.[9]

Either argument is usually buttressed with citation to a host of prior cases in which bankruptcy courts have allowed payments to critical trade vendors.[10] Of course, that veers somewhat near an "everyone-else-is-doing-it" sort of argument.

There is no doubt that paying some pre-bankruptcy claims – including those of employees and truly critical trade vendors – is often required if the debtor is to survive as a going concern. The law is just a bit shaky as to the basis for doing so.

ADMINISTRATIVE MATTERS

Another group of first-day motions addresses various housekeeping-type matters. One motion will typically ask the court to set a series of monthly, omnibus hearings for the course of the case. This allows the debtor, and its professionals, to know that they will be in bankruptcy court on a specified day each month.

If the debtor is a member of a group of related companies, all in bankruptcy, it will file a motion for the joint administration of the

---

8 To wit, the "six-month rule" and the "necessity of payment doctrine." These arguments are examined in detail in *In re Boston & Maine Corp.*, 634 F.2d 1359 (1st Cir. 1980). In short, the six-month rule allowed receivership courts to pay recent pre-bankruptcy claims ahead of secured claims on the theory that such claim had improved the secured creditors collateral, while the necessity of payment doctrine was addressed to "the more general authority of the receivership court to accord priority status to pre-receivership claims in order *to prevent the stoppage of a business impressed with the public interest.*" *Id.* at 1370 (emphasis added). That last, italicized point highlights the special status of railroads under American law.

9 *See* In re Kmart Corp., 359 F.3d 866, 872 (7th Cir. 2004).

10 All typically in unreported orders.

related cases. Strictly speaking, each legal entity within the corporate group has a separate bankruptcy case and, indeed, each one filed a separate chapter 11 petition. But it is not sensible to require each of them to file the same motion in each separate case. An order for the "joint administration" of related cases allows for a single motion to be filed in a lead case.[11]

Another typical motion sets up a procedure for the debtor to pay its non-bankruptcy professionals – for example, the attorneys who represent it in slip and fall cases around the country. Bankruptcy professionals – as we will discuss in Chapter 14 – are subject to court oversight, but surely the bankruptcy court has no desire to review every $4,000 bill from the lawyer who handles local use-tax issues in New Mexico.[12]

Moreover, the retention rules under the Code apply to professionals retained "to represent or assist the trustee [or debtor] in carrying out [their] duties under this title."[13] Arguably ordinary course business operations, even those that involve professionals, do not relate to the trustee or debtor's duties under the Bankruptcy Code.

UTILITIES

Another motion, under section 366, attempts to shape the debtor's relationship with utility companies. These motions are important for any debtor with multiple locations, and thus multiple utility accounts.

Section 366 of the Bankruptcy Code provides that:

---

[11] Joint administration is procedural only, and should be distinguished from substantive consolidation, when a court orders a group of related companies to be treated as a single bankruptcy estate. Substantive consolidation is most often used when there has been a failure to follow corporate formalities, such that what is technically a group of related companies should, in equity, be treated as if they were a single company.

[12] In re Johns-Manville Corp., 60 B.R. 612, 620 (Bankr. S.D.N.Y. 1986) ("The penumbra of the § 327(a) term 'other professional persons' is quite obviously not intended to cover without limitation all those persons of education, ability and accomplishment in any calling who may be regarded as professionals based upon considerations of societal, governmental or academic accreditation, or their own self-esteem.").

[13] Bankruptcy Code § 327(a). *See also* Bankruptcy Code § 1107.

a utility may not alter, refuse, or discontinue service to, or discriminate against, the trustee or the debtor solely on the basis of the commencement of a case under this title or that a debt owed by the debtor to such utility for service rendered before the order for relief was not paid when due.[14]

In other words, the phone and electric companies cannot turn off the phone and the lights, just because its customer filed a bankruptcy petition. But section 366 also provides that a utility may alter, refuse or discontinue service if the trustee or the debtor fails to "furnish adequate assurance of payment" within twenty days of the petition date (thirty days, in a chapter 11 case).

Section 366's legislative history indicates that its purpose was to protect debtors from immediate cancellation of utility service when the petition was filed, while at the same time providing adequate assurance to utility companies that debtors would continue paying for such services post-petition. The section reflects the 1978 enactment date of the Code and a world where there was only one phone company or electricity company in any part of the country.[15]

But frequently a debtor (and its related entities) will receive utility service from tens or hundreds of different utilities across the country. Thirty days is simply not enough time to negotiate the terms of "adequate assurance" with each. In this first-day motion, the debtor will typically ask the court to extend the thirty-day period, or enter an order finding that the amount of a deposit proposed by the debtor (or no deposit) is adequate, or provide some other form of relief.

---

[14]   "Utility" is not defined in the Bankruptcy Code.

[15]   In modern times, not only do utilities benefit from adequate assurance and setoff provisions in § 366, but in certain circumstances they also enjoy the safe harbor protections under § 556 and administrative expense priority under § 503(b)(9). The safe harbors for derivative contracts exempt derivatives from most aspects of the automatic stay, the debtor's § 365 powers, and the avoiding powers. Stephen J. Lubben, *The Bankruptcy Code Without Safe Harbors*, 84 AM. BANKR. L.J. 123 (2010). It is relatively easy to recast a utility supply contract as a utility swap or forward that is protected by the safe harbors. *See, e.g.*, MBS Mgmt. Serv. v. MXEnergy Elect., 690 F.3d 352, 357 (5th Cir. 2012) (electricity requirements contract was a forward contract); In re Nat'l Gas Distribs., 556 F.3d 247, 258 (4th Cir. 2009) (a forward contract may provide for actual physical delivery of a commodity, such as gas).

POST-PETITION FINANCING ("DIP LOANS")

Once these relatively routine motions are heard, the court will often hear one of the most important first-day motions: a motion to approve debtor-in-possession (or DIP) financing. Companies in financial distress often find that their need for liquidity goes up just as the availability of traditional financing goes down. An immediate, post-filing infusion of cash from DIP financing may help the debtor restore vendor and customer confidence in its ability to maintain its liquidity throughout the reorganization.

Many companies will file their chapter 11 petitions just as they default under their existing loans. These companies will often have negotiated the DIP financing terms before filing the petition, so that it can be approved by the court, at least on a preliminary basis, in a first-day order.

DIP loans are structured like other loans – for example, a large debtor might well have a syndicated DIP lending facility, often provided by some or all of its pre-petition lenders.[16] Frequently, pre-petition lenders will take the position that the only basis upon which they will provide a DIP facility is if the debtor "rolls up" (pays off) the lenders' pre-petition debt.[17] This is a controversial practice, and a judge's likelihood of approving a roll-up provision in a DIP order will depend on the ratio of new money coming in. The smaller the percent of new money, the less likely it is that it will get approved.

Section 364 permits a trustee (and thus a DIP) to obtain credit or incur debt if it meets certain conditions set forth in the statute. The section allows the debtor to incur both unsecured and secured debt (although DIP loans are almost always secured). The court, after notice and a hearing, can grant to a post-petition lender:

---

[16]   Historically, loans were structured as revolving credit facilities, but increasingly they may also be at least partially term loans.

[17]   Among other things, this means *all* amounts owed to these lenders becomes post-petition debt. This gives the DIP lenders powerful negotiating leverage because as post-petition debt their (administrative) claims cannot be "crammed down" under a chapter 11 plan. *See* Chapters 16 and 17.

- a superpriority[18] administrative claim against the debtor;
- a lien on the property of the bankruptcy estate that is not already subject to a lien;
- a junior lien on property of the estate that is subject to a lien; or
- a "priming" lien, one that is senior or equal to a preexisting lien on property of the estate.

The last option can lead to lots of litigation over adequate protection, and is the source of many of the roll-ups previously mentioned. It is much easier for the DIP and its new lenders to avoid a fight over priming by simply paying off the old lenders.

This first-day motion seeks approval of the DIP financing that the debtor has negotiated, either with its pre-petition lenders or with new lenders. Most often the DIP loan is approved on a preliminary or partial basis, with final approval coming at some latter point, after the formation of a committee.

A few debtors enter bankruptcy with some cash in the bank, but that cash might be subject to a lender's control. While in most cases the DIP is free to use its property in the ordinary course, without further court involvement, that rule is reversed in the case of cash. That is, only with court approval can the debtor use its cash that is "cash collateral."[19]

To use cash collateral (either consensually or non-consensually), a debtor must demonstrate that the secured creditor's interest in the collateral is adequately protected.[20] As we noted in Chapter 3, adequate protection aims to maintain the value of a secured creditor's collateral as of the petition date.

For example, where the lender's collateral is receivables, it is common for the lender to be granted a "replacement lien" on receivables generated post-petition. Such protection is significant

---

[18]   That is, having priority over all other administrative expenses, and the priority granted in § 507(b) for creditors who received "inadequate" adequate protection. This is the "super-duper priority" referred to in Chapter 4.

[19]   Cash collateral is defined as "cash, negotiable instruments, documents of title, securities, deposit accounts, or other cash equivalents."

[20]   Each secured creditor – whether its collateral is a dump truck or cash – is entitled to adequate protection, but only with regard to cash collateral must the debtor provide such protection *before* using the collateral.

because section 552 of the Bankruptcy Code cuts off any receivables lien as of the bankruptcy petition date, but the payments received on pre-petition receivables would be cash collateral (as the proceeds of collateral).

That said, it is typically in the interests of both lender and debtor to resolve this matter before the case is filed. For that reason, the cash collateral motion the DIP presents on the first day typically sets for an agreed program of adequate protection that the lender is willing to accept, at least for some interim period of time. In many cases the cash collateral arrangements and DIP loan are presented to the court in a single motion.

SUMMARY

Filing for bankruptcy, even under chapter 11, draws a line in time between pre- and post-bankruptcy claims. But to stabilize the debtor's business and allow it to enter chapter 11 with the least amount of disruption, it is often necessary to blur that line. Chapter 11 practice has developed a system of first-day motions that facilitate this process. While DIP lending and cash collateral matters are the subject of express provisions of the Code, many other first-day motions rely on something more like bankruptcy "common law."

13. Committees

Key concepts:

- The U.S. Trustee's role
- Committee role in the case
- Committees as representatives
- Ad hoc committees
- Retiree and chapter 7 committees

Committees were routinely formed in equity receiverships, while the 1898 Bankruptcy Act initially contained no mention of committees. The receivership committees were the subject of withering criticism from New Dealers, some of it justified.[1] For example, in a receivership of the Texas & Pacific Railroad in the 1880s, the lead committee's chairman was in frequent contact with representatives of the Gould family, the controlling shareholder. There is no indication the bondholders – who the committee purported to represent – knew about this.

Nonetheless, committees were folded into the bankruptcy process and today committees play a key role in larger chapter 11 cases.

Shortly after the filing of a chapter 11 case, the United States Trustee will hold a meeting (at least in larger cases) to form an official committee of unsecured creditors, and will usually select candidates from the list of the largest unsecured creditors filed with the debtor's bankruptcy petition.[2] Other committees – comprised of retirees or shareholders – are also possible, but less common. And

---

[1] For more on this, see Alfred B. Teton, *Reorganization Revised*, 48 YALE L. J. 573 (1939).

[2] Bankruptcy Code § 1102(b)(1).

in many smaller and mid-sized cases, the U.S. Trustee finds little to no interest among creditors in constituting any committees.[3]

Committees can be appointed under sections 705 or 1114, but they are most often appointed under section 1102. Under that section it is the U.S. Trustee, and not the court, that has the initial charge to "appoint a committee of creditors holding unsecured claims" and who may "appoint additional committees of creditors or of equity security holders" as the U.S. Trustee "deems appropriate."[4]

The court has an ability to order the creation of additional committees or a change in membership of existing committees, but committees are ultimately made up by the U.S. Trustee.[5] Indeed, courts have held that if the U.S. Trustee appoints an additional committee, the court does not have the authority to dissolve the committee.[6] That is, the court and U.S. Trustee have complementary but distinct roles in the formation of committees.

In larger chapter 11 cases, the basic committee of unsecured creditors is almost a given. Additional committees are not as common as they were in the early days of the Code. The most likely candidate for an equity committee is a case involving a publicly traded debtor that is arguably solvent, such that equity might be entitled to a recovery in the case. But these days many debtors have piles of secured, junior, and subordinated debt when they file, making any equity recovery unlikely.

A committee appointed under section 1102 has the powers and duties set forth in section 1103.[7] Under subsection (a), a committee may select and authorize the employment of professionals to

---

[3] The Small Business Reorganization Act of 2019, codified in subchapter V of chapter 11 – and discussed in Chapter 21 – does away with the appointment of a committee in cases that proceed under its provisions.

[4] In a partnership case, the U.S. Trustee may appoint a committee of limited partners but not a committee of general partners since the latter do not qualify as "equity security holders" as defined in § 101 of the Code.

[5] The U.S. Trustee has the discretion to appoint a prepetition committee of creditors as the committee in the chapter 11 case if the prepetition committee was fairly chosen and is representative of the interests of creditors. Bankruptcy Code § 1102(b)(1).

[6] In re Caesars Entertainment Operating Co., Inc., 526 B.R. 265 (Bankr. N.D. Ill. 2015).

[7] The 2005 amendments to the Code also added a duty in section 1102(b)(3). In re Refco Inc., 336 B.R. 187 (Bankr. S.D.N.Y. 2006). One can only guess why this was not added to section 1103.

represent or perform services for the committee.[8] The committee's professionals are paid out of the estate. Subsection (c) lists a committee's functions in a chapter 11 case.

Fifth on the list of functions is a kind of catch all – "perform such other services as are in the interest of those represented" – that also reminds us that committees are representatives of a larger class of creditors or shareholders. Indeed, a member of a committee owes a fiduciary duty to the class the committee represents.[9]

In many recent cases, and several older ones as well, a group of creditors has come together to form an "ad hoc" committee. These sorts of committees can be formed before or after the petition date. Sometimes the debtor will agree to pay the committee's expenses, but the committee has no statutory right to get such expenses paid.[10]

Section 1114 of the Code authorizes the appointment of a "retiree committee," in a case where the debtor wants to reduce its obligations to former employees. The retiree committee's task is to represent retirees in negotiating the extent (if any) of the reduction of retiree benefits. If a union can represent the retirees, the statute gives them first preference, but in the absence of a union, or if the union has conflicting interests (*e.g.*, the union represents current employees whose interests may differ from retirees' interests), a committee will be formed. In all other respects the committee looks like one formed under section 1102.

---

[8] *See* Chapter 14.

[9] Westmoreland Human Opportunities, Inc. v. Walsh, 246 F.3d 233, 256 (3d Cir. 2001) ("We have construed § 1103(c) as implying a fiduciary duty on the part of members of a creditor's committee, such as the present Unsecured Creditors Committee, toward their constituent members ... A committee member violates its fiduciary duty by pursuing a course of action that furthers its self-interest to the potential detriment of fellow committee members."). *See also* In re Spiegel, 292 B.R. 748 (Bankr. S.D.N.Y. 2003).

[10] Ad hoc committees might also attempt to receive compensation for making a "substantial contribution" to the case. Section 503(b)(3)(D) of the Bankruptcy Code grants administrative-expense priority for the "actual, necessary expenses" incurred by a creditor, among other entities, in making a "substantial contribution" in a case under chapter 11. In addition, section 503(b)(4) of the Code grants an administrative-expense priority for "reasonable compensation for professional services rendered by an attorney ... of an entity whose expense is allowable under" section 503(b)(3)(D) and "reimbursement for actual, necessary expenses incurred by such attorney." The Code neither defines "substantial contribution" nor sets forth criteria to be used in determining whether a substantial contribution has been made in a chapter 11 case.

Section 705 also allows for the creation of committees in chapter 7 – unsecured creditors that can vote for a candidate for trustee under section 702(a) are eligible to vote to form the committee.[11] And therein lies an important distinction: while chapter 11 committees are appointed by the U.S. Trustee, members of chapter 7 committees are elected. The election is held at the 341 meeting, discussed back in Chapter 8 of this book. As noted, chapter 7 committees are quite rare.

While a committee of creditors is permissive in a chapter 7 case, the formation of a committee of unsecured creditors in a chapter 11 case is mandatory.[12] Likewise, there are no provisions in chapter 7 for formation of equity committees.[13]

SUMMARY

Committees bring both positive and negative elements to the chapter 11 process. On the one hand, a robust committee acts as a real check on the otherwise quite powerful debtor-in-possession. And the ability to retain counsel, paid for by the estate, gives dispersed creditors a real voice in the case.

On the other hand, committees can also be a source of cost in the case – not only because they retain their own professionals, but also because they can drive up the debtor's costs. An aggressive committee sometimes functions as little more than an estate-funded holdup creditor.[14]

---

[11] The provision has its roots in practice under the old Bankruptcy Act. In re Fed'n Workers Credit Union, Inc., 354 F. Supp. 1206, 1208 (N.D. Ohio 1973). Courts have held the provision does not apply in SIPA brokerage cases. In re MF Glob. Inc., 462 B.R. 36, 41 (Bankr. S.D.N.Y. 2011). SIPA is discussed in Chapter 10.

[12] Assuming the creditors want a committee – the U.S. Trustee cannot compel service, of course.

[13] Section 705 also does not provide for the retention of committee professionals. In re Dominelli, 788 F.2d 584, 586 (9th Cir. 1986). *But see* In re DeLorean Motor Co., 821 F.2d 649, 1987 WL 37786 at *2 (6th Cir. 1987) (noting bankruptcy court had authorized committee's retention of professionals).

[14] *See* Oscar Couwenberg & Stephen J. Lubben, *The Costs of Chapter 11 in Context: American and Dutch Business Bankruptcy*, 85 AM. BANKR. L.J. 63, 80 (2011) ("Appointment of a creditors' committee in a bankruptcy case increases cost in two respects: first by the cost of the committee itself, and second by the increased cost associated with time the debtor's professionals spend interacting with the committee.").

14. Professionals

Key concepts:

- Retention
- Adverse interests
- Disinterestedness
- Interim and final compensation
- Administrative insolvency
- Carve-outs

Chapter 11 undoubtedly costs more than chapter 7, but that extra cost is the price creditors pay for the additional recovery they obtain in chapter 11.[1] Professionals, intimately involved in every aspect of the debtor's plan, represent a big part of the extra cost of chapter 11.

Under section 327 of the Bankruptcy Code, a trustee is authorized to retain "one or more attorneys, accountants, appraisers, auctioneers, or other professional persons." In chapter 7 the trustee sometimes retains a law firm – sometimes the trustee's own law firm.[2]

In chapter 11, the debtor retains at least one, and often two, law firms.[3] Accountants and financial advisers are also common. The

---

[1] Smaller creditors admittedly pay the cost involuntarily.

[2] Section 327(d) also provides for situations where the trustee is themselves attorney to the estate. *See also* Bankruptcy Code § 328(b). This assumes there are assets to distribute in the chapter 7 case, or litigation to conduct.

[3] For example, if a New York-based debtor files its case in Delaware, it would typically seek to retain both its big New York law firm as its primary counsel and local counsel in Delaware. Moreover, big law firms often have conflicts representing debtors against big financial institutions, so even if the New York debtor filed its case in New York, it might seek to retain "conflicts counsel." Another variation on this is "efficiency counsel" – a second (or third) firm retained to handle smaller matters, not cost-effectively addressed by the lead counsel. For example, a law firm where mid-level associates bill at $500 an hour, and partners at $1,000, will find it

committee (or sometimes – committees) will retain one or more law firms too, along with its own financial adviser. If there is an examiner, we get one more law firm, and maybe a financial adviser. And then the DIP lenders get their counsel fees paid, as do indenture trustees.

Section 327 further provides that any professional retained by the trustee (or DIP) must "not hold or represent an interest adverse to the estate" and must be "disinterested persons."[4] The latter is defined in section 101, while adverse interests are not.

Under section 101(14), "disinterested person" means a person that—

(A)   is not a creditor, an equity security holder, or an insider;
(B)   is not and was not, within two years before the date of the filing of the petition, a director, officer, or employee of the debtor; and
(C)   does not have an interest materially adverse to the interest of the estate or of any class of creditors or equity security holders, by reason of any direct or indirect relationship to, connection with, or interest in, the debtor, or for any other reason.

Part A thus disqualifies professionals who are creditors or share-holders.[5] Thus, a law firm with an outstanding receivable from the debtor probably cannot be retained as the debtor's bankruptcy counsel under section 327(a).[6] Similarly, if a single attorney at the firm owns shares in the debtor, the firm could have a problem being retained.[7]

---

difficult to sue to recover a $100,000 preference, without eating up most of the recovery in legal fees. However, such a firm might be best suited to reorganizing a complex capital structure.

[4]   Under § 322, and the provisions of chapter 7 cross-referenced therein, chapter 7 trustees must also be "disinterested persons."

[5]   "Creditor" is defined in § 101(10) and includes holders of claims, defined in § 101(5). Equity security is defined in § 101(16) and under § 10(17), "Equity security holder" is the holder of an equity security of the debtor.

[6]   Sometimes, in anticipation of the potential fees in the chapter 11 case, a firm with an outstanding unpaid bill will agree to waive its claim against the debtor, so as not to be a "creditor" at the time of filing.

[7]   In many cases, courts will consider the size of the holding and the role of the attorney in question. For example, arguably a junior associate who owns 100 shares

Both parts A and B disqualify certain past and present insiders. Insiders include officers and directors of the debtor, thus presenting a problem for law firms or banks when their employees sit on the boards of clients.[8]

Part C of the definition of "disinterested person" is a kind of catch-all provision that overlaps with section 327(a)'s prohibition on the retention of those with "adverse interests." Under section 101(C), a professional may not "have an interest materially adverse" to the estate or its claimants, while section 327(a) disqualifies a professional who holds "an interest adverse to the estate."[9]

If anything, the requirement under section 327 would appear to be somewhat broader, inasmuch as it is not qualified by a materiality standard, although it is limited to the estate, while the "disinterested person" version includes adversity to classes of claims and interests against the debtor and indirect interests. We might also note that section 327(a) covers representation, while the section 101 definition of "disinterested person" seems to apply when the professional more directly is adverse to the debtor or its parties in interest.

In short, under the "disinterested person" version of adverse interests, the scope is broader, but the conflict must be material. At least in theory, section 327 is narrower in scope but requires a lower standard for finding a conflict. It also covers client representations, whereas "disinterested person" covers direct conflicts. I say in theory, because it is clear that not all courts draw these sorts of fine distinctions, and a professional that needs to thread the needle through these provisions might find themselves disqualified based on little more than the court's general sense that something does not smell right.

As a general rule of thumb, section 327's "adverse interest" test picks up conflicts of interest that also would be problematic under non-bankruptcy law. For example, an attorney may not represent a

---

of Lehman Brothers should not disqualify the entire firm – especially if the associate can be "walled off" from the attorneys working on the case. The attorney cannot solve the problem by selling the shares before the bankruptcy without triggering insider trading concerns.

[8] Bankruptcy Code § 101(31).

[9] In re AroChem Corp., 176 F.3d 610, 623 (2d Cir. 1999).

creditor and a debtor in the same case. If the attorney is the recipient of a preference, the attorney may not represent the debtor that has a fiduciary duty to recover that preference for the benefit of all creditors.[10]

The disinterested tests then overlay a group of (apparently) *per se* rules based on situations where the professional's past or present interests are deemed to undermine the bankruptcy process.[11] In small business cases in particular, this will tend to drive a wedge between the debtor and its long-time counsel.

In chapter 11, section 1107(b) provides that a professional is not disqualified from employment solely because of prepetition employment by or representation of the debtor. This is a change from the normal rule in the Code, which reflects the traditional distinction between a debtor and the trustee. Of course, it makes sense that a chapter 7 trustee cannot retain the debtor's own counsel, because the debtor and the estate are quite distinct, but in chapter 11 the "trustee" normally is the debtor as DIP.

Similarly realistic is section 327(b), that provides for the continued payment of "in house" professionals without court authorization.

Section 327(e) creates an exception from the strict requirements of section 327(a), for attorneys working on a single, specified matter (or type of matter). For example, if Bogartco was party to a lawsuit before bankruptcy, it would clearly be more efficient for its counsel in that action to stay on the job, even if it might not be entirely "disinterested," than to require Bogartco to retain new counsel and pay to get it up-to-speed.

Section 327(e) allows Bogartco to keep its current counsel so long as the firm does not have "any interest adverse to the debtor or to the estate with respect to the matter" on which it is to be retained. In our example, Bogartco's counsel might not have a conflict with respect to the specific litigation, but it might have some other conflict (a claim against Bogartco for pre-petition fees? possible preference exposure; a seat on Bogartco's board? representation of another Bogartco creditor?) that would prohibit it from being retained as general bankruptcy counsel. The appointment still needs court approval, but the conflict rules are less stringent.

---

[10] For example, if the attorney had her outstanding invoices paid off on the eve of bankruptcy.

[11] *But see supra* note 8.

Section 1103(a) permits a committee appointed under section 1102 to employ professionals, subject to court approval. Although the provisions of section 1103 do not directly reference the requirements of section 327, section 1103(b) does provide that any professional retained by a committee "may not, while employed by such committee, represent any other entity having an adverse interest in connection with the case."[12] Thus the case law is apt to develop in parallel. Representing a creditor that is a member of the class represented by the committee is not automatically a problem, but many professionals will want to avoid it.

In all cases, the debtor (or committee) must file an application to retain its chosen professionals, and the court must approve it.[13] The retention of professionals is supported by an extensive disclosure process.[14]

A retention application must disclose any connections between the professional and other parties to the case.[15] Only with full disclosure can the court decide if the requirements of the Code have been satisfied.[16] Professionals also have an ongoing obligation of disclosure – which includes a requirement that all disclosures be updated throughout the course of the case. Looming over the entire process is the famous criminal case of *United States v. Gellene*,[17] in which a prominent New York City bankruptcy attorney was convicted of filing a false disclosure declaration and sentenced to fifteen months in federal prison.

Under section 328(a), the court sets the terms of the retention, including the terms of compensation, at the point of retention. Those terms can only be varied later "if such terms and conditions prove to have been improvident in light of developments not capable of being anticipated at the time of the fixing of such terms

---

[12] The disinterestedness requirement does not apply.
[13] Note that this is a retention application, signed by the client, rather than a motion signed by the client's attorney.
[14] One of these disclosure requirements is that a professional's application for employment under Bankruptcy Code § 327(a) "shall be accompanied by a verified statement of the person to be employed setting forth the person's connections with the debtor, creditors, any other party in interest, their respective attorneys and accountants[.]" *See* Bankruptcy Rule 2014.
[15] Bankruptcy Rule 2014.
[16] In re Citation Corp., 493 F.3d 1313, 1321 (11th Cir. 2007).
[17] 182 F.3d 578 (7th Cir. 1999).

and conditions." Thus, the court might agree that partners will charge $1,000 per hour, associates $500 per hour, and paralegals $150. Those hourly rates are set for the duration of the case – although the total number of hours the professionals can actually bill in the case will be set through the compensation system.[18]

After the court has approved professional's retention, the next hurdle it faces is getting paid. Section 331 permits professionals to file interim fee applications every 120 days while the case is pending, with one final fee application at the end.[19] In large cases, a typical first-day motion asks the court to enter an order authorizing the debtor to pay some percentage of its and the committee's professionals' fees and expenses (often, 90 percent of fees and 100 percent of expenses) on a monthly basis. As a result, the interim and final fee applications are really about approving retroactively the fees paid, and authorizing the payment of amounts withheld.

In reviewing fee applications, section 330(a)(1) instructs the bankruptcy judge to approve

(A) reasonable compensation for actual, necessary services rendered by the trustee, examiner, ombudsman, professional person, or attorney and by any paraprofessional person employed by any such person; and

(B) reimbursement for actual, necessary expenses.

---

[18] Section 328(a) has been the source of confusion among the courts, particularly in cases where setting the terms of compensation also greatly influences the amount of compensation. At the end of the case, it may be difficult to analyze the "reasonableness" of a financial adviser's compensation, as required by § 330 (discussed below). But under § 328(a), the court can modify the terms of the adviser's compensation only if they appear excessive in light of circumstances not "capable of being anticipated at the time of the fixing of such terms." Bridling under this restriction on their discretion, courts sometimes say § 328(a) applies only when that section is expressly flagged in the retention application – that is, if the professional sought to be retained "under section 328(a)." But the Code contains no such requirement, and arguably the better interpretation is that all professionals are retained under § 327, and modifications of their compensation is subject to § 328(a). In short, the terms of retention should be subject to serious consideration at the point of retention, and not second-guessed with the benefit of hindsight. For more on this issue, see Stephen J. Lubben, *The Chapter 11 Financial Advisors*, 28 EMORY BANKR. DEV. J. 11, 27 (2011) ("the case law analysis of the interrelationship between §§ 327(a), 328(a), and 330 is nothing short of an intellectual mess.").

[19] Bankruptcy Code § 331.

Section 330(a)(3) then provides a laundry list of things the court might consider in deciding what is reasonable. Throughout the court retains the ability to deny what it deems to be unreasonable compensation, or requests to reimburse for unnecessary expenses.

The court also has the ability to deny compensation to any professionals who should not have been retained in the first instance.[20] Courts have interpreted this power to include an ability to claw back compensation paid to professionals who failed to disclose matters relevant to the analysis under section 327(a), even if those matters would not have resulted in denial of retention. That is, failure to disclose is itself grounds for reduction in compensation.

Professionals might also be compelled to return previous compensation in cases of "administrative insolvency." For example, in *Specker Motor Sales Co. v. Eisen*, the Sixth Circuit Court of Appeals affirmed a bankruptcy court order that a chapter 11 debtor's attorney had to disgorge some of the fees awarded before the case was converted to chapter 7, because the estate lacked sufficient funds to pay all administrative claims in full.[21] The attorney's pro rata share of the estate was less than $1,000. However, because he had already been paid $10,000 (a retainer, which the court had allowed the attorney to offset against an outstanding bill as interim compensation), the bankruptcy court ordered the attorney to disgorge the portion of the retainer in excess of the pro rata distribution mandated by section 726(b) of the Bankruptcy Code.[22]

On the other hand, while many courts have allowed disgorgement in such cases, it is questionable whether they would order a similar remedy against another administrative claimant that was paid during the course of the bankruptcy case. For example, if a trade

---

[20] Bankruptcy Code § 328(c).

[21] 393 F.3d 659 (6th Cir. 2004).

[22] Other courts have held that pre-petition retainers are not subject to disgorgement. In re Yoo, 339 B.R. 730, 739 (B.A.P. 9th Cir. 2006) ("Neither the Sixth Circuit (nor the district court nor the bankruptcy court) considered the issue of whether the professional held a security interest in the retainer funds thereby protecting the retainer from section 726(b) disgorgement."). The Sixth Circuit's conclusion to the contrary may have been motivated by the fact that Bays received his retainer after Specker filed for bankruptcy, but the opinion does not appear to make any distinction between pre- and post-petition retainers.

creditor was paid on an invoice for materials the debtor no longer needed after shutting down, would the court order the vendor to return the payment? If not, there needs to be some reason to explain the different treatment.[23] Courts should also consider that while disgorgement might achieve equity in a particular case, the long-run effects could be pernicious.[24]

Another risk may be more common: all of the estate's assets are covered by a secured creditor's (or even more likely, DIP lender's) lien. If there is no estate equity in the collateral, having a first-priority administrative claim is meaningless. The professionals are first in line to receive nothing.

To deal with this risk, professionals often negotiate a "carve-out" to provide for payment of their allowed fees. The carve-out is essentially an agreement by the DIP lender to permit some specified amount of fees to come first in line in terms of payment from the estate's assets. Negotiating such an agreement does place the professional (especially attorneys) in an awkward situation, where they are jointly representing the debtor's interests and their own interests.[25]

SUMMARY

Outside of bankruptcy, professional compensation and ethics are largely policed by professional rules and after-the-fact litigation. In the communal bankruptcy forum, is it thought that such a *laissez faire* approach is inappropriate. Indeed, we might worry that the DIP, and perhaps the committee, lack the appropriate incentives to monitor professionals that are paid from the larger estate. In some

---

[23] For a case that comes close to offering such an explanation, see In Re Saint Catherine Hospital of Indiana, LLC, 2018 WL 4620273, at *5 (S.D. Ind. Sept. 26, 2018) ("the 'value' of services rendered by counsel must take into account all relevant circumstances, and administrative insolvency is relevant.").

[24] In re Home Loan Serv. Corp., 533 B.R. 302, 305 (Bankr. N.D. Cal. 2015) ("If disgorgement of interim fees were a real possibility in all chapter 11 cases due to post-conversion chapter 7 administrative insolvency, then that policy could have a serious chilling effect on chapter 11. The chapter 11 professionals would likely respond by demanding larger up-front retainers ...").

[25] Of course, there is an inherent (if often unacknowledged) tension between attorneys and their clients on the issue of fees in general. *See* Jay L. Westbrook, *Fees and Inherent Conflicts of Interest*, 1 AM. BANKR. INST. L. REV. 297 (1993).

sense bankruptcy professionals might be more aptly analogized to plaintiff's counsel in corporate derivative litigation, who also have their fees reviewed by trial courts.

15. The plan – formulation and voting

> **Key concepts:**
>
> - Exclusivity
> - Mandatory and optional plan provisions
> - Classification
> - Voting and impaired classes
> - Securities laws and plans
> - Adequate information

Plans are the key goal of most chapter 11 cases. A chapter 11 reorganization or liquidation plan is in essence a contract.[1] A great big, giant contract.

These plans could either reorganize the debtor or distribute the proceeds of an earlier sale of the debtor. The plan might even provide for the liquidation of the debtor, providing an alternative to chapter 7.[2] The Code provides a detailed set of rules for formulating these court-imposed contracts we call "plans."

Upon the commencement of a chapter 11 case, Bankruptcy Code section 1121 gives a DIP the exclusive right to file a plan for 120 days. The DIP also has the exclusive right to solicit votes on a plan filed within that 120-day period until 180 days after the petition

---

[1] Ernst & Young LLP v. Baker O'Neal Holdings Inc., 304 F.3d 753, 755 (7th Cir. 2002).

[2] Bankruptcy Code § 1123(b)(4). *See* Bankruptcy Code § 1141(d)(3)(A); In re FMO Associates II, LLC, 402 B.R. 546 (Bankr. E.D.N.Y. 2009) ("Courts have recognized that where liquidation would proceed more expeditiously and less expensively under the control of the debtor, conversion from Chapter 11 to Chapter 7 may not be warranted.").

date.[3] No competing plans may be filed during this period without court permission or the occurrence of certain itemized conditions.[4]

Section 1121 gives the bankruptcy court the discretion to either extend or reduce the debtor's "exclusivity" upon a showing of "cause." But the 120-day period during which the DIP has the exclusive right to file a chapter 11 plan "may not be extended beyond a date that is 18 months" after the petition date. In addition, the 180-day period during which only the DIP may solicit votes for a plan may not be extended beyond twenty months after the filing date.[5]

Thus, at least as an initial matter, the debtor will typically take the lead in drafting a plan. But the outlines of the plan – likely beginning with a term sheet, which may have been negotiated even before the petition was filed – will be the subject of negotiations with key creditor constituencies like DIP lenders, pre-petition lenders, union representatives, and official and *ad hoc* (*i.e.*, non-court appointed) committees.

Section 1123(a) of the Bankruptcy Code lists the mandatory provisions of a chapter 11 plan, and section 1123(b) then provides the discretionary provisions. Fundamentally, section 1123(a)(1) states that a chapter 11 plan must designate classes of claims and interests for treatment under the reorganization. Under that provision, the debtor will allocate its capital structure to various classes, always with one eye on the fact that chapter 11 plans are accepted or rejected by class.

As a result, Bogartco might carefully consider whether it is better to put all of its bondholders in a class with other unsecured creditors, like trade and tort creditors, or separately classify business and investment creditors. The company may not classify solely to gerrymander, but most courts would allow such separate classification with a sufficient business reason (like Bogartco's need to maintain a relationship with trade creditors after reorganizing). Likewise, while bondholders might be happy to receive equity in

---

[3] Roughly four and six months, if you want to match the days of the first part of the rule to the months of the second part, discussed below. Not exactly fine statutory drafting there.

[4] Among these are the appointment of a trustee and the debtor's failure to file a plan or obtain acceptance of a plan within the exclusive periods.

[5] Before 2005, the court could extend exclusivity indefinitely, and many debtors had exclusivity throughout their time in chapter 11.

the reorganized Bogartco, trade creditors would likely prefer payment in cash, and that might support separate classification.

Section 1122(a) of the Bankruptcy Code provides that "a plan may place a claim or an interest in a particular class only if such claim or interest is substantially similar to the other claims or interests of such class."[6] It does not say what "substantially similar" means. That is left to case law, along with the question of separately classifying similar claims.

It is customary to separately classify each secured claim. Thus, the bank with the first mortgage on Bogartco's plant will be in one class, while the hedge fund with the second mortgage will be in another class. But if a group of investors share a single lien on assets, they should be classified together – absent some good business reason for separate classification.

Under section 510(a) of the Bankruptcy Code, subordination agreements are enforceable to the extent they are enforceable under applicable non-bankruptcy law, which can lead to separate classification. For example, Bogartco's subordinated bondholders should be separately classified from the senior bondholders, even though they are both unsecured creditors in a broad sense.

Application of section 506(a) to the claim of a secured creditor is potentially altered in a chapter 11 case by the provisions of section 1111(b) of the Code.[7] For students and bankruptcy novices, 1111(b) ranks as amongst the most confusing of the business bankruptcy provisions in the Code.

Section 1111(b)(1) first provides that a secured claim is allowed or disallowed just as if the holder of the claim had recourse against the debtor,[8] whether or not such recourse would otherwise be available under state law. That is, even non-recourse loans become

---

[6] Section 1122(b), in turn, provides that "[a] plan may designate a separate class of claims consisting only of every unsecured claim that is less than or reduced to an amount that the court approves as reasonable and necessary for administrative convenience." The class consists of unsecured claims below a certain threshold dollar amount, which, as a result of their "convenience claim" status, may often (though not always) be paid quickly, in cash, in full – even though their larger-sized counterparts in other unsecured classes may receive an entirely different plan treatment.

[7] Refer back to Chapter 4 for a discussion of § 506.

[8] That is, an ability to assert a supplemental unsecured "deficiency" claim, if the collateral does not cover the debtor's full obligations.

recourse loans in chapter 11, and the creditor is entitled to a two-part claim under section 506.[9]

Turning back the other direction, section 1111(b)(2) allows a secured creditor to opt out of section 506's bifurcation of their claim, and instead treat its claim only as secured.[10] The secured creditor gives up its unsecured deficiency claim – the product of either its contract or section 1111(b)(1), as discussed above – in exchange for retaining its original lien at full face value.

This "1111(b) election" is attractive to a secured creditor who believes that the property that secures the debt is (temporarily) undervalued by the market, undervalued by the court, or that the reorganized firm is likely to default again in the near future. The tradeoff is that, by making the election, the creditor losses its voting power as an unsecured creditor and will receive no recovery on the deficiency claim under the plan.

Ultimately, the creditor must weigh the return to unsecured creditors under the plan against the expected value of future appreciation in the collateral. By making the election, and keeping the lien in place, that future appreciation will go to the creditor, instead of the debtor or the estate generally.

Imagine a bank with a lien on Bogartco's warehouse. The building is worth $600,000, but Bogartco owes $1 million. Under the normal 506 rule, this creditor would have two claims under the plan: a secured claim for $600,000 and an unsecured claim for $400,000. The bank would vote in each class, but after confirmation of the plan, its lien would be reduced to $600,000.[11] And Bogartco could get the property free of the lien by paying the creditor $600,000.

---

[9] The special treatment of a non-recourse loan terminates if the property securing the loan is sold under § 363 or is to be sold under the plan. The ability to make the § 1111(b) election, discussed below, terminates in these situations as well.

[10] Strictly speaking, § 1111(b) is phrased in terms of a class, and the class must vote (by the usual two-thirds in amount and 50 percent in number standard) to make an 1111(b) election. But because secured creditors are so often in a class by themselves, it is easier to think of this in terms of the election being personal to the creditor.

[11] *See* Bankruptcy Code § 1129(b).

If the bank instead makes the 1111(b) election, its claim would be $1 million.[12] It would only vote as a secured creditor, and it will retain its lien on the warehouse in the full, original amount of $1 million. As noted, the election make sense if the bank thinks that Bogartco is taking advantage of a dip in property values, or if the bank thinks that Bogartco's plan will never work – and thus, it will be useful to have the full lien when the case converts to chapter 7 or is dismissed.

Interests – that is, equity interests – are also classified. Thus, all business debtors will have at least one class of interests, but if Bogartco has issued preferred stock in addition to its common stock, it will have two classes.

Thus, to comply with 1123(a)(1), Bogartco's plan might look something like this:

- Class 1: First Mortgage Holders
- Class 2: Second Mortgage Holders
- Class 3: General Unsecured Creditors
- Class 4: Senior Bondholders
- Class 5: Subordinated Bondholders
- Class 6: Preferred Shareholders
- Class 7: Common Shareholders

That would be relatively simple. Below in Table 15.1 we see another example: the classification structure from the Lehman Brothers chapter 11 plan. And this is only for the holding company: there were classification schemes for each of the American subsidiaries too.

---

[12]   That is, the nominal amount of the claim will be $1 million. As discussed in the next two Chapters, that amount might be paid over time. Thus, sometimes the creditor will not want to make the election, because partial payment on the deficiency claim has a higher present value than payment in full over an extended period of time.

Table 15.1 Summary of classification and estimated recovery of claims and equity interests under the plan[1]

Lehman Brothers Holdings Inc. ("LBHI")

Class	Type of Claim or Equity Interest	Estimated Recovery[2]	Impairment; Entitlement to Vote
1	Priority Non-Tax Claims	100%	Impaired, Entitled to Vote
2	Secured Claims	100%	Impaired, Entitled to Vote
3	Senior Unsecured Claims	21.1%	Impaired, Entitled to Vote
4A	Senior Affiliate Claims	15.6%	Impaired, Entitled to Vote
4B	Senior Affiliate Guarantee Claims	15.2%	Impaired, Entitled to Vote
5	Senior Third-Party Guarantee Claims	12.2%	Impaired, Entitled to Vote
6A	Convenience Claims	26.0%	Impaired, Entitled to Vote
6B	Convenience Guarantee Claims	17.0%	Impaired, Entitled to Vote
7	General Unsecured Claims	19.9%	Impaired, Entitled to Vote
8	Affiliate Claims	14.4%	Impaired, Entitled to Vote
9A	Third-Party Guarantee Claims other than those of the Racers Trusts	11.5%	Impaired, Entitled to Vote
9B	Third-Party Guarantee Claims of the Racers Trusts	7.0%	Impaired, Entitled to Vote
10A	Subordinated Class 10A Claims	0%	Impaired, Not Entitled to Vote, Deemed to Reject
10B	Subordinated Class 10B Claims	0%	Impaired, Not Entitled to Vote, Deemed to Reject
10C	Subordinated Class 10C Claims	0%	Impaired, Not Entitled to Vote, Deemed to Reject
11	Section 510(b) Claims	0%	Impaired, Not Entitled to Vote, Deemed to Reject
12	Equity Interests in LBHI	N/A	Impaired, Not Entitled to Vote, Deemed to Reject

Notes:

1 Further detail regarding the Estimated Recoveries set forth in the below table is included in the Recovery Analysis and notes thereto annexed hereto as Exhibit 4.

2 With respect to each of the Debtors, where the Estimated Recovery percentage is shown as "N/A," the amount of Estimated Allowed Claims in such Class is zero dollars.

Section 1123(a) also requires that the plan set forth whether or not a particular class is impaired by the plan, and precisely what the class' treatment will be. We see that on Table 15.1, where the table indicates both matters. For example, we can see that class 7 general unsecured claims will receive an approximate 20 percent recovery, and are impaired and entitled to vote.[13]

Class 12, the shareholders, are receiving nothing and are impaired, but are not entitled to vote. To understand why, we need to understand "impairment" as defined in the Code, and then section 1126's voting rules, which include two rules for "automatic" voting by certain classes.

Under section 1124, a class is unimpaired by a plan when it "leaves unaltered the legal, equitable, and contractual rights to which such claim or interest entitles the holder of such claim or interest." In short, if the class retains all the rights it had before bankruptcy, it is unimpaired. That said, the Code does allow the debtor to "unwind" the effects of acceleration clauses. For example, imagine Bogartco's bonds, normally due in ten years, became due and payable before bankruptcy because it missed an interest payment. If Bogartco cures the default, it can still treat this class of bondholders as unimpaired if it commits to pay according to the indenture going forward.

If a class is actually unimpaired – sometimes they will debate the point – section 1126 provides that they are presumed to vote in favor of the plan. That is, if you are getting paid in full, in complete accordance with your rights, we do not want to hear you complain. Such a class is automatically deemed to vote in favor of the plan.

The other automatic voting rule comes from the other end of the treatment distribution: classes that receive absolutely nothing are automatically deemed to reject the plan. This is the fate of the Lehman Brothers shareholders, noted above. It is the fate of common shareholders in many chapter 11 plans.

Everyone in between – that is, classes that are impaired but are receiving some recovery – get to vote. Under section 1126(c) of the Bankruptcy Code, such a class of claims is deemed to accept a plan

---

[13]   Unsecured creditors were initially slated to recover 21 cents on the dollar when Lehman's liquidation plan went into effect in 2012. However, they have since recovered nearly twice that amount as Lehman's liquidation has brought in more money than expected.

if the plan is accepted by creditors that hold at least two-thirds in amount *and* more than one-half in number of the allowed claims in the class.[14]

This two-part voting rule is designed to keep large creditors from dominating the class, while still recognizing that those with the largest amount of money on the line should have an important voice. If you understand this voting rule you can understand many of the considerations that go into classification: can Bogartco get two-thirds of the senior bondholders to vote for the plan? If not, would it be better to combine the unsecured creditors in a single class and obtain two-thirds of that group?

Only the holder of an *allowed* claim is entitled to vote.[15] Similarly, only those claim holders who have actually voted are considered when calculating acceptance under section 1126(c).

Section 1126(e) permits the court to designate (disallow) the votes of any entity whose acceptance or rejection of a plan was not in good faith or was not solicited or procured in good faith. Discussing section 203 of chapter X of the Bankruptcy Act, the predecessor of section 1126(e), the Supreme Court explained that "[t]he history of this provision makes clear that it was intended to apply to those ... whose selfish purpose was to obstruct a fair and feasible reorganization in the hope that someone would pay them more than the ratable equivalent of their proportionate part of the bankrupt assets."[16]

Increasingly, in larger chapter 11 cases, debtors and creditors execute "lock-up agreements" that set forth the terms of a plan of reorganization and bind creditors who execute such agreements to vote in favor of the plan, subject to satisfaction of the terms of the

---

[14]   A class of equity interests accepts a plan if the plan has been accepted by interest holders "that hold at least two-thirds in amount of the allowed interests of such class held by holders of such interests ... that have accepted or rejected such plan."

[15]   Allowance is determined by reference to section 502. If there is no proof of claim on file, the claim may nonetheless be treated as though such a claim were on file if it is listed in the debtor's schedules (unless it is listed as disputed, contingent or unliquidated). Bankruptcy Code. § 1111(a). *See* Chapter 4.

[16]   Young v. Higbee Co., 324 U.S. 204, 210-11 (1945).

lock-up agreements.[17] Under the agreement, the promise to vote is typically enforceable by specific performance.

In order to prevent a fight over nonconsensual confirmation (cramdown),[18] a plan proponent may include a "death trap" provision that will incentivize an impaired class to vote for the plan by providing a distribution, or a larger distribution than it otherwise would receive.[19] For example, if the bondholders vote in favor of Bogartco's plan, they get 25 percent of the equity in the reorganized company, while if the class votes against the plan, they get 10 percent of the equity.[20]

Returning to section 1123, another commonly used provision is subpart (a)(5)(J), which allows the debtor to issue securities in exchange "for cash, for property, for existing securities, or in exchange for claims or interests, or for any other appropriate purpose." This provision works hand-in-hand with section 1145, which provides a targeted exemption from federal and state securities laws.

In short, section 1145(a) provides an exemption from the registration requirements of the Securities Act of 1933, and similar state laws, for securities distributed to existing creditors or shareholders under a chapter 11 plan. Section 1145(b) also contains a special definition of "underwriter," that replaces the broader definition in

---

[17] Sometimes these "lock ups" are part of a larger restructuring support agreement (or "RSA"), signed before the bankruptcy petition is filed. Creditors will often seek to include a provision requiring the debtors to seek swift approval from the Bankruptcy Court to (a) assume a prepetition RSA (under Bankruptcy Code § 365) or (b) enter into and perform under a post-petition RSA (under Bankruptcy Code § 363).

[18] *See* Chapter 17, *infra*.

[19] In re Adelphia Commc'ns Corp., 368 B.R. 140, 275–76 (Bankr. S.D.N.Y. 2007) ("This 'carrot and stick' provision, by which a creditor is offered an inducement to vote on a plan of reorganization, is not inconsistent with any provision of the Code—though I'd prefer to qualify that general statement to make it applicable if (but only if) the inducement is to give a stakeholder more than it would be entitled to, rather than to threaten to take an existing right away.") (footnote omitted).

[20] In re Zenith Elecs. Corp., 241 B.R. 92, 105 (Bankr. D. Del. 1999) (explaining that the "Plan provides that if Bondholders do not accept it, they will receive nothing under the Plan and the Plan proponents will seek cramdown pursuant to section 1129(b) as to them. In contrast, if the Bondholders accept the Plan, they will be entitled to a pro rata distribution of $50 million of the new 8.19% Senior Debentures.").

the Securities Act, and thus allows greater resale of securities received under a plan. Furthermore, under section 1145(c), any such distribution of securities under a plan is considered to be a public offering, providing more flexibility for subsequent resale than would be the case if the issuance were considered an exempt private offering (such as private placements under Rule 144A of the Securities Act).[21]

Once the plan is drafted, it can only be sent out for a vote with a court-approved disclosure statement.[22] The court must find that the disclosure statement contains "adequate information," that is, information "that would enable ... a hypothetical investor of the relevant class to make an informed judgment about the plan." Courts have developed long laundry lists of what must be included in a disclosure statement.

Solicitation of votes with a court-approved disclosure statement provides an exemption from other potentially relevant laws – again, think of federal and state securities laws – that might require a greater degree of disclosure.[23] Nonetheless, it is common to attach a recent 10-K as an exhibit to the disclosure statement of publicly traded debtors.[24] In many cases, where the disclosure statement is

---

[21]   And § 1145(d) provides an exemption to the Trust Indenture Act of 1939 for short-term debt instruments – with a maturity of less than a year – distributed under the plan.

[22]   Bankruptcy Code § 1125(b).

[23]   Bankruptcy Code § 1125(e). *See also* id. at § 1125(d); Yell Forestry Prods., Inc. v. First State Bank of Plainview, 853 F.2d 582, 584 (8th Cir. 1988) ("[W]e feel that the purpose of section 1125(e) would be defeated if an action could be maintained against a proponent for common law fraud in the sale of securities pursuant to a plan of reorganization."). Importantly, section 1125(e) protects only a plan proponent that solicits in good faith.

[24]   *E.g.*, In re U.S. Brass Corp., 194 B.R. 420, 424-25 (Bankr. E.D. Tex. 1996):

Case law under § 1125 of the Bankruptcy Code has produced a list of factors disclosure of which may be necessary to meet the statutory requirement of adequate information. The relevant factors for evaluating the adequacy of a disclosure statement may include: (1) the events which led to the filing of a bankruptcy petition; (2) a description of the available assets and their value; (3) the anticipated future of the company; (4) the source of information stated in the disclosure statement; (5) a disclaimer; (6) the present condition of the debtor while in Chapter 11; (7) the scheduled claims; (8) the estimated return to creditors under a Chapter 7 liquidation; (9) the accounting method utilized to produce financial information and the name of the accountants responsible for such information; (10) the future management of the debtor; (11) the Chapter 11

drafted as a comprehensive, standalone document, this allows the creditors to read the same basic information about the debtor twice.[25]

SUMMARY

A chapter 11 plan is a contract imposed on all of the debtor's creditors and other claimants. In this Chapter we have seen how the debtor normally has "first crack" at drafting such a plan, and how the terms of the plan and the voting thereon are structured by the Bankruptcy Code. As we will see in the coming Chapters, classification and voting are closely tied to the question of whether the debtor's plan will be consensual or necessitate the use of the Code's "cramdown" power to adopt the plan against the wishes of one or more dissenting classes.[26]

---

plan or a summary thereof; (12) the estimated administrative expenses, including attorneys' and accountants' fees; (13) the collectibility of accounts receivable; (14) financial information, data, valuations or projections relevant to the creditors' decision to accept or reject the Chapter 11 plan; (15) information relevant to the risks posed to creditors under the plan; (16) the actual or projected realizable value from recovery of preferential or otherwise voidable transfers; (17) litigation likely to arise in a nonbankruptcy context; (18) tax attributes of the debtor; and (19) the relationship of the debtor with the affiliates.

[25] Better practice is to draft a "slim" disclosure statement, that incorporates the 10-K by reference. But that makes some law firm partners twitchy.

[26] Bruce A. Markell, *Clueless on Classification: Toward Removing Artificial Limits on Chapter 11 Claim Classification*, 11 Bankr. Dev. J. 1, 2 (1995) ("*Classes* vote. An impaired *class* must accept. Only dissenting *classes* in a cramdown receive the benefit of the fair and equitable and no unfair discrimination rules.") (emphasis in original).

16. The plan – confirmation (consensual)

> **Key concepts:**
>
> - Good faith
> - Best interests of creditors
> - Voting and blocking positions
> - Feasibility

Once a chapter 11 plan has been sent to creditors, and those creditors vote on the plan under section 1126,[1] the court must then consider the plan under section 1129. This is the "confirmation" process.[2]

Section 1129(a) sets forth sixteen confirmation requirements that the plan must satisfy if all classes of creditors have voted to accept the plan (but not all sixteen apply to every plan). That process – called "consensual confirmation" – is the subject of this Chapter. The court may also confirm the plan over the objection of one or more dissenting classes, if the plan meets the requirements in section 1129(b) (which, in addition to its own requirements, incorporates many of those in section 1129(a)). Confirmation over the objection of one or more classes is called "cramdown" and is the subject of Chapter 17.

Note that in rare cases, if the debtor has been unable to either file a plan or to garner sufficient support for its plan before the

---

[1] *See* Chapter 15. Recall that under Bankruptcy Code § 1126(c), a plan must be accepted by: (1) a majority of creditors within a class (the "numerosity" requirement); and (2) creditors holding at least two-thirds of the value of the claims within a class.

[2] The term likely comes from the old railroad receiverships, where the court had to "confirm" the results of the foreclosure sale, and thus implement the agreed-upon plan.

expiration of its exclusivity periods,[3] another party may file a competing plan. In that case, creditors may vote on competing plans, and the bankruptcy court will hold a confirmation hearing to determine which (if either) to confirm. Under section 1129(c), however, the court may confirm only one plan, which seems sensible.

We take the key elements of section 1129(a) in order.

Sections 1129(a)(1) and 1129(a)(2) require that the plan and the plan proponent comply with the applicable provisions of the Bankruptcy Code – in other words, that the plan meets the requirements of sections 1122 and 1123 relating to plans (discussed in Chapter 15) and that the proponent has performed its duties under the Code.

The Code next requires that the plan be presented in "good faith."[4] In addition to being proposed in good faith, a plan must not be proposed by "means forbidden by law." Given that section 1129(a)(1) already contains a specific requirement that the plan comply with the Code, section 1129(a)(3)'s requirement must be that the plan must comply with *other* applicable law – including state law – beyond the Bankruptcy Code. To take an extreme example, Bogartco could not use the chapter 11 process to convert itself into a depository bank, despite the normal rules for chartering such a bank.

Section 1129(a)(4) requires the court approve all the debtor's payments of expenses and costs made in connection with the bankruptcy case. Typically this involves professional fees, and confirms the court's authority over bankruptcy professionals up until the point the estate ceases to exist, and the debtor resumes normal operations.[5]

The Code then requires the proponent to disclose the identity and affiliations of any individual proposed to serve, after confirmation, as a director, officer, or voting trustee of the debtor.[6] The plan proponent must also disclose any insider who will be employed or

---

[3] *See* Chapter 15.

[4] Under Chapter X of the old Bankruptcy Act, "good faith" was a prerequisite for court approval of a Chapter X petition, rather than a plan.

[5] *See* Chapter 14.

[6] Bankruptcy Code § 1129(a)(5)(A)(i).

retained by the reorganized debtor and the nature of any compensation for that insider.[7]

The appointment to or continuance in office of any individual who is going to serve as a director, officer, or voting trustee, must be "consistent with the interests of creditors and equity security holders and with public policy." This may preclude the retention of pre-bankruptcy management, forcing a governance change at this point. Many jurisdictions force such a change at the outset of an insolvency case, through the appointment of a trustee, but consistent with the debtor-in-possession model, in chapter 11 these issues are left to the plan process.

Section 1129(a)(6) applies to debtors in regulated industries, and provides such regulators with a role in the plan process. For example, a utility company might require regulatory approval for a new rate structure, and subsection (a)(6) acknowledges that authority and conditions approval of the plan on approval of the rate structure.

Section 1129(a)(7) applies in all cases. It provides that each creditor or interest holder who votes to reject the plan (even if their class voted to accept) must receive, on the plan's effective date, at least as much as they would receive if the debtor were liquidated on that date. That is, all dissenting parties must get at least as much in chapter 11 as they would in a hypothetical chapter 7 of the same debtor. Chapter 7 thus acts as a floor to chapter 11 plans.

The test in section 1129(a)(7) is known as the "best interests of creditors" test, and as noted it focuses on individual dissenting creditors, rather than classes.[8] An individual holder can object to the plan on the basis that the reorganization is not in the holder's best interests, as liquidation of the debtor would yield more value for its claim.

In determining whether the plan satisfies the test, the bankruptcy court will assess the liquidation analysis in the disclosure statement,

---

[7]   Bankruptcy Code § 1129(a)(5)(B).

[8]   Section 1129(a)(7) represents a codification of the judicial gloss placed on the "best interest of creditors" provision that applied to the confirmation of plans under chapter XI of the old Bankruptcy Act. Under § 366(2) of chapter XI of the Act, a plan that was not approved by every creditor in each class had to be in the "best interests of creditors" to be confirmed. The "best interests" test was interpreted to require that creditors receive something more than they would receive in a liquidation.

which details the recoveries of each class of claims and interests in a hypothetical chapter 7 liquidation. Thus, the plan proponent will need to retain an expert who can value the debtor for chapter 7 purposes, and make that expert available to testify at the confirmation hearing.

A different standard applies to the dissenting holder of a secured claim that is part of a class that has made the section 1111(b) election, and thus is treated solely as a secured creditor, notwithstanding section 506.[9] (Remember that in most cases, each secured creditor will be in its own class). In that case, each holder of a secured claim within such a class must receive a recovery that is no less than the value of the creditor's collateral.

In short, the creditor must receive value equal to at least the secured portion of the claim under section 506 – even if section 506 claim bifurcation does not apply because of the 1111(b) election. There is no 1111(b) election in chapter 7, so this revised rule looks to what the creditor would actually get in chapter 7: the value of the collateral when sold by the trustee.

Next we turn to section 1129(a)(8), which requires that *all* impaired classes accept the plan. If this requirement is not met, the debtor will have to use the cramdown provisions of 1129(b).[10] Remember that classes that receive nothing under the plan automatically reject it, so in such a case cramdown will be inevitable.[11] In many cases the elimination of old shareholders or subordinated debtholders will thus necessitate cramdown.

Section 1129(a)(9) addresses treatment of claims entitled to priority treatment under section 507(a) of the Code. The section addresses priority claims in four different ways.

Under section 1129(a)(9)(A), each allowed administrative claim must be paid in full in cash on the plan's effective date, unless the

---

[9]   *See* Chapter 15 for a discussion of the § 1111(b) election.

[10]   There is a split in authority on whether a class of creditors who have failed to vote should be considered to have accepted the plan, but probably the majority of courts have found that a class must actually vote to accept a plan to be considered an accepting class.

[11]   Bankruptcy Code § 1126(g) ("a class is deemed not to have accepted a plan if such plan provides that the claims or interests of such class do not entitle the holders of such claims or interests to receive or retain *any property* under the plan on account of such claims or interests.") (emphasis added).

holder agrees otherwise. This means, perhaps not surprisingly, that the chapter 11 lawyers and other professionals always get paid, in full, as soon as their fees are approved.

Administrative insolvency and the inability to meet this requirement, as noted in Chapter 14, is a frequent motivation for conversion to chapter 7 or dismissal of the case. For example, if the debtor's assets are sold and the secured creditors take all of the proceeds, the debtor will be unable to meet the requirements of 1129(a)(9)(A).

Then under section 1129(a)(9)(B), the plan must provide that claims relating to wages and employee benefit plans, along with certain consumer deposits, must either be paid in cash on the effective date of the plan or, if they vote to accept as a class, they can receive deferred cash payments with a present value equal to the value of their claims. That is, either they get paid in full on the effective date of the plan, or they get interest on their claims to compensate them for the delay in payment. The latter option is only available if the class of such claims consents to the plan – a dissenting class will have to be paid on the effective date. In many larger chapter 11 cases this section will be a non-issue, since these sorts of creditors will have been paid under a first-day motion and order.[12]

Section 1129(a)(9)(C), which covers priority tax claims, is similar, but it limits the length of payment to five years. That is, while the debtor might pay employee wage claims over a decade – provided the plan provides for a high enough interest rate – the taxing authorities must be paid within five years. Taxing authorities, perhaps in recognition of their sovereignty, are also treated individually, and not on a class basis.[13]

On the other hand, payment over five years is available to the debtor even if the taxing authorities reject the plan.[14] It bears noting that section 1129(a)(9)(C) only applies to pre-petition tax claims –

---

[12] *See* Chapter 12.
[13] Note that while § 1129(a)(9)(B) mentions the class, § 1129(a)(9)(A) and (C) speak about the holder of claims.
[14] But the language requiring the payments to be made in regular installments and in a manner not less favorable than the most favored nonpriority unsecured claims, other than administrative convenience claims under Code § 1122(b), means that priority tax claims cannot be paid over five years if the general unsecured creditors will be paid in three.

post-petition claims might well be entitled to priority treatment as administrative expenses under section 1129(a)(9)(A).[15]

Section 1129(a)(10) of the Bankruptcy Code requires the affirmative acceptance of a plan by at least one class of impaired claims, "determined without including any acceptance of the plan by any insider." In an ideal world, this section and section 1129(a)(8) would appear together, because each relates to the other, but section 1129(a)(9) somehow got stuck in the middle. Section 1129(a)(10) is the narrower of the two: it requires *one* impaired class to accept.

Section 1129(a)(10) applies in a cramdown – at least one impaired class needs to accept before you can attempt a cramdown. Somebody has to like the plan.

That, of course, might tempt the debtor to create a class that is both likely to accept the plan and every-so-slightly impaired. Some case law prevents blatant attempts in this regard, but debtors with subtlety will find this an important part of plan formulation.

Although a debtor's efforts to rig the vote to secure confirmation remain subject to the "good faith" requirement of section 1129(a)(3), a "good faith" challenge is likely to be costly to litigate and the outcome unpredictable. Perhaps more common in recent cases have been moves by creditors to obtain "blocking positions" within classes, which prevent a plan from meeting either of the section 1126(c) requirements referenced above. For example, a creditor can block acceptance of a plan if it holds just over one-third of the value within a class, which sometimes can be a worthwhile investment if the creditor holds a sizable stake in some other part of the capital structure.[16]

Here is where the "death trap" provisions discussed in Chapter 15 come into play. If the death trap successfully gets at least one class to agree to the plan, cramdown can be invoked because the terms of section 1129(a)(10) are satisfied.

We then turn to section 1129(a)(11), which is often referred to as the "feasibility test." The test requires the court to make an

---

[15]　In re Scott Cable Communications, 227 B.R. 603 (Bankr. D. Conn. 1998).

[16]　Likewise, if the creditor base is relatively concentrated, it may be possible to buy more than half of the claims by number, but representing only a small dollar value. In re Fagerdala USA-Lompoc Inc., 891 F.3d 848 (9th Cir. 2018) (secured creditor, owed $4 million, purchased $13,000 in claims, representing about 10 percent of total value of unsecured claims but more than half of the total number of such claims).

independent determination as to whether the plan is workable and has a realistic likelihood of success.

Just how probing the court's review on this point should be – particularly in the absence of any concerns by those parties with real money on the line – is a point of serious contention among bankruptcy academics and practitioners. In a nutshell, to establish the feasibility of a reorganization plan, the debtor must present reasonable projections that there will be sufficient cash flow to fund the plan and maintain operations according to the plan, and such projections cannot be utterly speculative or unrealistic.[17]

Plans that fail this requirement most often assume certain events will happen that are not within the debtor's control. For example, a plan that depends on financing that has yet to be obtained might fail under section 1129(a)(11). Likewise for a plan that presumes a governmental permit not yet obtained.

Section 1129(a) has five other requirements, largely ministerial. If the debtor is subject to a collective bargaining agreement and has a large number of retirees covered by a retirement health plan, section 1129(a)(13) may be important. It provides that the plan must provide for the continuation of "retiree benefits," as defined in section 1114 (typically, benefits provided under a retiree health plan) at the pre-bankruptcy level, unless the court has authorized a modification of those benefits under the special provisions of section 1114.[18]

We close with a brief mention of section 1129(d), which is not strictly speaking a confirmation requirement. Nonetheless, it might provide the basis for a court to refuse to confirm a plan that is a bit too clever. Section 1129(d) provides as follows:

> Notwithstanding any other provisions of this Section, on request of a party-in-interest that is a governmental unit, the court may not confirm a plan if the principal purpose of the plan is the avoidance of taxes or the avoidance of the application of section 5 of the Securities Act of 1933. In any hearing under this subsection, the governmental unit has the burden of proof on this issue of avoidance.

---

[17] Pan Am Corp. v. Delta Air, Inc., 175 B.R. 438, 508 (S.D.N.Y. 1994).
[18] *See* Chapter 5.

In short, the chapter 11 process should not be used to further tax avoidance, or end-runs around the securities laws. This provision is only enforceable by regulators, but it is important to remember whenever you start to feel that chapter 11 is a solution to every debtor-firm's business or regulatory problems.

SUMMARY

This Chapter has worked through the key provisions of section 1129(a), which provides the basis for consensual confirmation of a plan. Most of these requirements also apply when a plan is confirmed under section 1129(b), the cramdown power discussed in the next Chapter. Among the most frequently litigated by objecting creditors are the requirement, under section 1129(a)(7), that the creditors get at least as much as they would in chapter 7 (the "best interests" test) and the requirement, under section 1129(a)(11) that the plan be "feasible."

17. The plan – confirmation (cramdown)

Key concepts:

- Cramdown
- Unfair discrimination
- Fair and equitable
- The absolute priority rule

The word "cramdown" is bankruptcy lingo for confirmation of a plan in the face of creditor objections.[1] In summary, to achieve confirmation by cramdown, Bankruptcy Code section 1129(b) requires that the plan be "fair and equitable" as to each dissenting class, and also that the plan not "unfairly discriminate" against a dissenting class. In addition, the plan must comply with most provisions of section 1129(a).[2]

Confirmation of a plan without the consent of all classes is thus possible, but subject to specific rules. Section 1129(b)(1) sets forth the requirements.

---

[1]   The term "cramdown" (the noun, the verb is "to cram down") seems to have first been used to describe similar provisions, added to § 77 (railroad reorganization) of the Bankruptcy Act in 1935. Warner Fuller, *The Background and Techniques of Equity and Bankruptcy Railroad Reorganizations–A Survey*, 7 LAW & CONTEMP. PROBS. 377, 390 (1940) ("Under the amended Act a plan of securities readjustment may become binding on dissenting classes of creditors or stockholders, even though they are offered no alternative of cash payment for their interests in the old company (§77e). These so-called "cram-down" provisions may be invoked, however, only where the court finds, after hearing, that the reorganization plan makes adequate provision for the dissenters' interests and that their rejection of the approved scheme of securities readjustment is not reasonably justified."). *See also* Robert T. Swaine, *Present Status of Railroad Reorganizations and Legislation Affecting Them*, 1940 SEC. COMM. L. 15, 15 (1940).

[2]   Bank of America National Trust and Sav. Ass'n v. 203 North LaSalle Street Partnership, 526 U.S. 434, 441 (1999).

The plan must comply with all elements of section 1129(a), except the requirement that *all* impaired classes accept. This means that at least one impaired class must accept the plan, even if all other impaired classes have rejected the plan. Think of this as a "somebody has to like it" rule.

That is, while cramdown gets the plan proponent (often the debtor) out from the requirement of section 1129(a)(8), it still must comply with subsection (a)(10), which requires that any plan with an impaired class be approved by at least one class of claims that is impaired under the plan, without giving any effect to the votes of insiders.[3] The plan must also meet the best-interests-of-the-creditors test, comply with the Bankruptcy Code and other relevant laws, be presented in good faith, and otherwise comply with every subpart of section 1129(a), other than 1129(a)(8).

As noted, section 1129(b)(1) then articulates two additional tests that a plan proponent must satisfy to confirm a plan over the dissent of a rejecting class. First, the plan must not "discriminate unfairly." Second, the plan must be "fair and equitable."

The Code does not define what is meant by the phrase "discriminate unfairly." The phrase seems to suggest that some degree of discrimination is permissible, so long as it does not cross a line and become *unfair*.[4]

It is typically thought that unfair discrimination is a horizontal equity test. It ensures that a plan does not favor a class having comparable priority to the dissenting class simply because the favored class voted for the plan, and the dissenting class did not.[5] More generally, it also prevents attempts to pick favorites, harming some creditors while benefiting others, without some good reason for doing so.

---

[3] Thus even if a class formally approved the plan, if the margin in favor of approval included insiders, the plan may have trouble meeting the requirements of § 1129(a)(10).

[4] For example, imagine that under the debtor's plan, unsecured trade creditors will receive 20¢ on the dollar, and unsecured bondholders will receive new bonds with a value equal to 20 percent of their old bonds. The two classes have equal priority, but they will receive different treatment. But this discriminatory treatment is not "unfair" – trade creditors want cash, bondholders are used to holding investment securities.

[5] In re Armstrong World Indus., Inc., 348 B.R. 111, 121 (D. Del. 2006).

This connects with the classification concerns we discussed in prior Chapters. Not only might a debtor classify similar creditors in distinct classes to meet the requirements of section 1129(b)(1) and its incorporation of section 1129(a)(10), but the debtor might simply want to treat some creditors better than others.

For example, Bogartco might owe $5 million to Gutman Industries and likewise to Cairo Incorporated, each on an unsecured basis. Bogartco might justify putting the Gutman claim in a separate class because the debtor needs to maintain a good relationship with Gutman post-bankruptcy. That would provide a good business reason for separate classification under section 1122, but if the plan were structured with a provision that provided that Cairo's recovery would be 90 percent if it votes for the plan, and 60 percent if it votes against the plan, while Gutman gets 90 percent no matter what, that would be unfair discrimination.[6]

The Code does not prohibit separate classification. But separate classification does not get the debtor or Gutman anything. It is the separate treatment that is problematic or discriminatory.

But note that the discrimination issue only becomes relevant if Gutman rejects the plan. Cairo can consent to its treatment, in which case section 1129(b)'s special tests become irrelevant because we are back in the land of section 1129(a) and consensual confirmation.

Other common fact patterns of unfair discrimination include plans that pay the unsecured portion of a secured lender's deficiency claim at a lower rate than all other unsecured creditors, or plans that put all the risk of the reorganized business on a class that does not want to take such risk.

In contrast, the "fair and equitable" test in section 1129(b)(1) – whether a plan is "fair and equitable" as to a dissenting class – is said to be a vertical equity test. Section (2) of subsection (b) defines the phrase "fair and equitable" as it applies to various dissenting classes – secured claims, unsecured claims, and interests (equity). Historically the test as applied to unsecured creditors was where most of the action was, but with the increasing use of multiple

---

[6] Bruce A. Markell, *A New Perspective on Unfair Discrimination in Chapter 11*, 72 AM. BANKR. L.J. 227 (1998).

layers of secured debt in companies' capital structure, the treatment of secured claims has also made important appearances in recent cases.

Section 1129(b) provides that a plan is "fair and equitable" with respect to a dissenting class of unsecured claims if either (i) the dissenting class is paid in full (including interest, if payment is made over time), or (ii) no class junior to the dissenting class receives anything under the plan on account of their junior claims or interests. In other words, creditors must be paid in full before shareholders receive anything. This rule is called the "absolute priority rule."[7]

But what if the old shareholders get equity in the reorganized firm not because they were shareholders in the old, bankrupt company, but because they bought the new equity with cash? In other words, is there an exception to the absolute priority rule if, under the plan, shareholders receive equity in the reorganized company in exchange for "new value" provided to the company?

The fusing of the phrase "fair and equitable" to both the "absolute priority rule," and the so-called New Value Exception to the rule,[8] has its roots in late 1939, when the Supreme Court, speaking through Justice Douglas in *Case v. Los Angeles Lumber Products Co.*, handed down its first decision actually interpreting the "fair and equitable" language in a case arising under the by then repealed section 77B.[9] Douglas had just joined the Court in 1939, after a career as both an academic and an important member of the SEC staff, ultimately serving as its third chairman.[10]

---

[7]   In keeping with Voltaire's quip about the Holy Roman Empire, the Absolute Priority Rule has "been criticized … as being none of those three things (absolute, about priority, or a rule)." Jonathan C. Lipson, *Directors' Duties to Creditors: Power Imbalance and the Financially Distressed Corporation*, 50 UCLA L. Rev. 1189, 1229 (2003).

[8]   Sometimes also called the "New Value Corollary." Bank of Am. Nat. Tr. & Sav. Ass'n v. 203 N. LaSalle St. P'ship, 526 U.S. 434, 446 (1999).

[9]   Case v. L.A. Lumber Prods. Co., 308 U.S. 106 (1939). Section 77B was the first general corporation reorganization provision to be federally codified. It was replaced in the late 1930s with Chapters X and XI, which were added to the Bankruptcy Act. Both Roman numeral chapters were replaced with chapter 11 of the current Bankruptcy Code in 1978.

[10]   Justice Brandeis retired February 13, 1939; Justice Douglas was confirmed as his successor on April 4, 1939.

In his years with the SEC, he had been actively involved with the drafting of a multi-volume report[11] in which the agency blasted the equity receivership system for favoring insiders at the expense of small bondholders.[12] This report not only prompted the Chandler Act, which thoroughly revised corporate bankruptcy, but also the Trust Indenture Act of 1939, which made it quite difficult to reorganize bond debt outside a federal bankruptcy proceeding.[13] Justice Douglas personally lobbied his colleagues to grant certiorari in *Los Angeles Lumber* presumably to continue the work he had started with the SEC.[14]

In the case itself, holders of more than 92 percent of the debtor's bonds along with more than 99 percent of Class A stock and about 90 percent of Class B stockholders approved the debtor's reorganization plan. But the plan provided for bondholders to be transformed into preferred shareholders, and Class A shareholders to become the new common shareholders.[15] In short, Class A shareholders would retain their interest in the company in a situation where everyone agreed that the bondholders were not being paid in full. Justice Douglas wrote that:

> the phrase ["fair and equitable"] became a term of art used to indicate that a plan of reorganization fulfilled the necessary standards of fairness. Thus throughout the cases in this earlier chapter of reorganization law, we find the words "equitable and fair", "fair and equitable", "fairly and equitably treated", "adequate and equitable", "just, fair, and equitable" and like phrases used to include the 'fixed principle' of the *Boyd* case, its antecedents and its successors. Hence we conclude, as have other courts, that that doctrine is firmly imbedded in [Section] 77B.[16]

---

[11] *See* Securities And Exchange Comm'n, Report on the Study and Investigation of the Work, Activities, Personnel and Functions of Protective and Reorganization Committees (1937–1940).

[12] J. Ronald Trost, *Corporate Bankruptcy Reorganizations: For the Benefit of Creditors or Stockholders?*, 21 UCLA L. Rev. 540, 542–44 (1973).

[13] *See* Caplin v. Marine Midland Grace Trust Co. of N.Y., 406 U.S. 416, 422 (1972).

[14] Kenneth N. Klee, Bankruptcy and the Supreme Court 378–79 (2008).

[15] Class B shareholders were eliminated.

[16] Case v. L.A. Lumber Prods. Co., 308 U.S. 106, 118-19 (1939) (footnotes omitted).

The question, he said, was whether the debtor's plan was fair. He concluded it was not because the bondholders "will be required under the plan to surrender to the stockholders 23 per cent of the value of the enterprise."[17] Suggesting that "fair and equitable" had become "term of art" in the railroad receivership community exaggerated things more than a bit.[18] But here we see the linking of "fair and equitable" to the absolute priority rule, although even Douglas does not actually use the words "absolute priority rule."

Indeed, in the same case, Justice Douglas recognized that railroad receiverships had routinely allowed old shareholders to buy into the reorganized railroad without violating the "fair and equitable" (or absolute priority) rule, and he indicated that would continue to be the case going forward.[19] He observed that "[w]here that necessity exists and the old stockholders make a fresh contribution and receive in return a participation reasonably equivalent to their contribution, no objection can be made." The modern foundation of the New Value Exception was born.

By the late 1970s, times had changed, and the absolute priority rule that once protected small investors as bondholders now hurt them as shareholders.[20] Thus, the new 1978 Code limited the application of the absolute priority rule to contested confirmations, and narrowed its applicability to secured creditors, as we will soon discuss.

But did the New Value Exception survive?

That is the subject of some debate, to put it mildly. As the Seventh Circuit explained:

> The new value precept, though mentioned in the Bankruptcy Commission's report to Congress, was not expressly codified in the Bankruptcy Code of 1978 ... Whether it survives the enactment of the new Code is

---

[17]   *Id.* at 119.

[18]   In the words of Jack Ayer: "Strictly speaking, this is poppycock, and Justice Douglas knew it." John D. Ayer, *Rethinking Absolute Priority After Ahlers*, 87 MICH. L. REV. 963, 975 (1989); *see also* De Forest Billyou, *"New Directions": A Further Comment*, 67 HARV. L. REV. 1379, 1380–81 (1954).

[19]   In *Consolidated Rock Products Co. v. DuBois*, Justice Douglas made it plain that the absolute priority rule applied to Chapter X too. Consol. Rock Prods. Co. v. DuBois, 312 U.S. 510 (1941).

[20]   *See* 124 CONG. REC. 34,004 (1978); *see also* Lynn M. LoPucki & William C. Whitford, *Bargaining over Equity's Share in the Bankruptcy Reorganization of Large, Publicly Held Companies*, 139 U. PA. L. REV. 125, 133 (1990).

the subject of much debate. The current trend is to treat the new value precept not as an exception (as it was commonly called) but as a corollary to the absolute priority rule preserved in the 1978 Code.[21]

That is, most courts assume it still exists, but maybe with a slightly different name. In *Bank of America National Trust & Savings Ass'n v. 203 North LaSalle Street Partnership*,[22] the Supreme Court studiously avoided answering the basic question, while holding that "plans providing junior interest holders with exclusive opportunities free from any competition fall within the prohibition of § 1129(b)(2)(B)(ii)." In short, assuming the exception does still exist, other classes must be allowed to try to get the new equity – the old shareholders may not get an "inside track." Specifically, the Supreme Court found the absolute priority rule is violated by a plan "provision for vesting equity in the reorganized business in the Debtor's partners without extending an opportunity to anyone else either to compete for that equity or to propose a competing reorganization plan."[23]

Turning to secured creditors, a plan is "fair and equitable" with regard to a dissident class – or a secured creditor, who are often classified in a class by themselves – if one of three alternative conditions is satisfied.

First, the debtor can give the secured creditor an IOU[24] with a principal amount equal to the current value of the collateral, with that value secured by the collateral, and a market interest rate. If the creditor chooses to make the "fully-secured" election under section 1111(b), not only will the debtor have to give an IOU with a principal amount equal to the collateral value and a market interest rate, but the total payments of principal and interest over the life of the plan must equal at least the face amount of the secured creditor's debt. And the creditor gets to keep its full lien on the

---

[21]   In re Woodbrook Assocs., 19 F.3d 312, 320 (7th Cir. 1994).

[22]   526 U.S. 434 (1999).

[23]   Some circuits (*e.g.*, the Seventh) require actual auctions of the new equity – although there is little support for such a requirement in *LaSalle* itself. Others simply require that plan exclusivity be lifted upon the filing of a New Value plan. In some cases, the court will compare the new value being paid against the value of the shares, as indicated by a discounted cash flow analysis or other common valuation technique. *See* In re Red Mountain Mach. Co., 448 B.R. 1, 18 (Bankr. D. Ariz. 2011), *aff'd*, 471 B.R. 242 (D. Ariz. 2012).

[24]   That is, a new debt instrument.

collateral until it is paid – that is, the lien is not "stripped down" to the current collateral value.

In the first case the creditor gets payments with a present value equal to the collateral; in the second case, under 1111(b), the creditor gets the same present value, but the total nominal payments have to match the face amount of the debt.[25] In either case, a key point of dispute will often be if the debtor is paying a sufficiently high interest rate on the claim, necessary to meet the present value requirements for cramdown.[26]

Second, the debtor can sell the creditor's collateral, and give the creditor a lien on the sale proceeds. The creditor will have a right to "credit bid" its full secured claim in the sale, so that this option might result in the debtor giving the creditor its collateral in exchange for debt relief.[27]

The third and final option is referred to as "indubitable equivalent." The phrase comes from an old Learned Hand decision, although knowing that does little to help understand its actual meaning.[28] In short, the debtor is given an opportunity to argue that the creditor is being made whole, but it is a demanding standard, and often not met.[29] The one situation where "indubitable equivalence" is routinely found is when the debtor gives the lender back its collateral in satisfaction of the debt. This looks a bit like option two, discussed above, without any actual sale of the collateral.

Then we come to the shareholders. Section 1129(b)(2)(C) provides that equity can be crammed down if the equity is either paid

---

[25]   In the first case the creditor also has an unsecured claim for the deficiency, but its lien can be cut down to the collateral value. In the second case, the creditor forgoes its deficiency claim to retain its original lien. See the discussion of the 1111(b) election in Chapter 15 of this book.

[26]   *See generally* Thomas S. Green, *An Analysis of the Advantages of Non-Market Based Approaches for Determining Chapter 11 Cramdown Rates: A Legal and Financial Perspective*, 46 Seton Hall L. Rev. 1151 (2016).

[27]   RadLAX Gateway Hotel, LLC v. Amalgamated Bank, 566 U.S. 639, 649 (2012).

[28]   In re Murel Holding Corp., 75 F.2d 941 (2d Cir. 1935). *See also* Bankruptcy Code § 361(3).

[29]   The most common use of the provision is under plans that give creditors real property in exchange for release of debt secured by some other property. If the creditor rejects the proposed "dirt for debt" exchange, the question is whether the property offered provides the "indubitable equivalent" of the creditor's old loan. In re Sugarleaf Timber, LLC, 529 B.R. 317, 335 (M.D. Fla. 2015).

what it is entitled to, or no junior class is receiving any recovery. This is comparable to the treatment of unsecured creditors.

Two issues can arise with regard to cramdown of equity. First, a class of preferred shares might argue that they are entitled to more, before the common shares can receive anything.

Second, and more commonly, common shareholders will often argue that the plan undervalues the debtor, and creditors are being overcompensated at the expense of equity – for example, in a plan that proposes to eliminate the common stock and distribute new equity to unsecured creditors. In that case, shareholders may argue that the new equity is worth more than the unsecured claims, and that some of the new equity should go to them.

So long as the plan proponent can present valuation evidence showing that equity is entirely "out of the money," cramdown in these situations is relatively easy, as there are no junior classes to the common shares.[30]

Cramdowns of common shareholders are commonplace in large business bankruptcy cases. But in smaller cases, where the existing shareholders desperately want to keep control of the business, they will make every effort to reach a consensual confirmation.[31] Creditors have some incentive to reach a consensual deal too, because a small business is apt to lose much value if the founders choose to walk away.

SUMMARY

Cramdown is the process for approving a plan that has some support, but which has been rejected by one or more classes. Some cramdowns are straightforward, particularly those involving the elimination of common equity interests. Others are more complex, particularly where a secured creditor contends that it is not receiving proper value for its claim.

---

[30] The equity class is deemed to have rejected the plan under Bankruptcy Code § 1126(g).

[31] When consent was impossible, these are the sorts of cases that historically made frequent use of the New Value Exception. Going forward, they will probably proceed under subchapter V whenever the debtor qualifies. *See* Chapter 21.

While the special "fair and equitable" and "unfair discrimination" tests are important in cramdown, it is equally important to remember that the general section 1129(a) provisions are also applicable, with the sole exception of section 1129(a)(10).

18. 363 sales

In some cases, and perhaps with greater frequency in the past two decades or so, debtors find it easier to sell their assets in the early days of the case, and then turn to negotiating a plan that will distribute the proceeds.[1] In essence this plan becomes a liquidating plan, and an important part of the action occurs at the point of the sale.[2] These sales are referred to as "363 sales," after section 363 of the Code.

Sometimes a debtor files for chapter 11 and expects to do a 363 sale, because that is what will best preserve its value. For example, if the debtor's business will suffer more than usual damage while in bankruptcy, it might make sense to sell the assets as a going concern in the early days, and get the operations out of bankruptcy quickly. In other cases, the debtor will plan on doing a quick 363 sale because it has no other viable choice. In many cases prepetition lenders offer DIP financing for a short period of time. The debtor has no realistic choice but to do a quick 363 sale, before that financing expires.

---

[1]   The ABI Commission to Study the Reform of Chapter 11 has expressed particular concern about the speed of sales of all or substantially all of a debtor's assets, and has proposed moratorium on these sales for the first sixty days of a case. To date Congress has not taken up this proposal.

[2]   If the debtor is unable to confirm a plan after the sale – perhaps the sale proceeds belong to the secured lenders, leaving nothing to pay administrative claims – the case might convert to chapter 7.

And in other cases, plan negotiations bog down, perhaps with some creditors pushing for one valuation of the company, while others point to a much lower number, and the debtor finds that a 363 sale is the only way to get the operating company out of bankruptcy in a timely fashion.[3] The debtor might have survived a chapter 11 of normal length, but an extended stay in bankruptcy begins to wear on the business.

Section 363(b)(1) simply provides that the "trustee, after notice and a hearing, may use, sell, or lease, other than in the ordinary course of business, property of the estate."[4] That is, unless it is an ordinary course transaction, any sale, use or lease of estate property needs court approval. Such a sale can include most of the debtor's assets, leaving the debtor (and the estate) as little more than a corporation that holds the sale proceeds.

But section 363(b) itself provides little guidance on how such a whole debtor sale should happen. Bankruptcy Courts have filled the void, and a fairly complex "common law" set of procedures have developed to structure such sales.

The 363 sale process often begins even before the petition date, with a traditional, corporate-law sale process. Investment bankers will contact potential bidders, and attempt to sign up one as the "stalking horse."[5] The stalking horse bidder is the lead or favored bidder, who will end up with the debtor's assets if no other bidders emerge through the sale process. The stalking horse bidder also benefits from an ability to shape the general outline of the sale, even if other bidders do arise, since the initial asset purchase agreement is typically used as the model for all bidders that follow.

This lead bidder will often want to negotiate a "break-up fee," to compensate it for its time and expense if it gets outbid in the process. But bidders should keep in mind that a pre-bankruptcy break-up fee agreement is subject to being rejected by the debtor under section 365, and a post-bankruptcy agreement is itself subject

---

[3] The Adelphia Communications Corporation bankruptcy (filed in 2002) provided an example of this sort of case.

[4] Remember that under § 1107 we can read "DIP" for trustee here when dealing with a chapter 11 case.

[5] According to the *Oxford English Dictionary*, the term comes from the sixteenth century, "from the former practice of using a horse trained to allow a fowler to hide behind it, or under its coverings, until within easy range of prey." Something for bidders to keep in mind.

to the terms of 363(b) – that is, it needs bankruptcy court approval. Thus, bidders will want to get the break-up fee in front of the court in the early days of the case, perhaps at the first-day hearing. So long as the fee is modest, and not so large as to have an obvious effect on bidding, bankruptcy courts tend to approve them.[6]

Approval of the break-up fee will frequently be folded into a larger motion asking the court to approve of the debtor's proposed process for conducting the sale.[7] In the motion, the debtor will describe its prepetition marketing process, the agreement it has reached with the stalking horse bidder, and how the debtor proposes to conduct an auction to seek "higher and better" offers. This bidding procedures motion will ask the course to approve things like the size of deposits that bidders have to provide, the bidding increments at the auction, and the date and time of the auction.

The sale procedures motion will also set up the process by which the court will approve the sale itself, including objection deadlines and how objectors will be able to investigate the debtor's pre-bankruptcy sale process. A hearing to approve the sale will also be set at this time. As noted, none of this is set forth in section 363 itself, but has developed over time, particularly in jurisdictions like Delaware and the Southern District of New York, where the courts handle complex 363 sales with some frequency.

Under section 363(k), an existing secured lender has the right to credit bid at a 363 sale, meaning that the prepetition lenders are potential sources of competing bids. In some cases, they might even be the stalking horse bidder. This is particularly true if the loan is made by or ends up in the hands of non-traditional lenders, such as hedge funds and private equity firms, who might have an investment interest in the debtor's assets.

The ultimate goal of the process is to maximize return to the estate, and as a result, the court can override its previously approved bidding procedures and accept late or non-conforming bids. Knowledge of this flexibility, and also because of the limited time frame to conduct due diligence, might dissuade some bidders from participating in the 363 process in the first instance. That is, it

---

[6]   The typical fee is between 1 and 3 percent of the final sales price. It is also important to disclose all the permutations in which the fee might be paid. In re Energy Future Holdings Corp., 2018 WL 4354741, at *10 (3d Cir. Sept. 13, 2018).

[7]   In re Innkeepers USA Tr., 448 B.R. 131, 146 (Bankr. S.D.N.Y. 2011).

is not always clear that speed and flexibility of the process actually achieves the desired goal.

The asset purchase agreement must be filed in the bankruptcy court along with the sale motion explaining the terms of the agreement and seeking approval of the sale. That is, the process involves two motions: a procedures motion and a motion to actually approve the final deal.

The sale agreement itself looks like asset purchase agreements used outside of bankruptcy. But because the debtor is insolvent or at least in significant distress, the purchaser cannot expect to derive any real protection from representations, warranties or indemnification. Rather, the sale is effectively "as is." The agreement may also provide that the debtor will assume and assign certain contracts that the purchaser needs to keep the business running.[8]

Any contracts not assumed, and any assets not sold, remain in the estate to be dealt with as part of the chapter 11 plan process. For debtors with some "bad" assets mixed in with other "good" assets – say a toxic waste site owned by an otherwise viable business – this ability to sort the assets is quite valuable.[9]

Section 363(m) of the Bankruptcy Code provides that a purchaser who purchases assets in good faith cannot have a transaction unwound on appeal even if the appellant obtains a reversal of the order approving the 363 sale. Thus, a purchaser will often want the sale order to include a finding from the bankruptcy court that it is a good faith purchaser.

When a debtor seeks to sell all of its assets under a 363 sale, a common objection is that the debtor is short-circuiting the more elaborate safeguards of the confirmation process, including the duty to provide adequate information (in a disclosure statement) to parties in interest. In the 1980s, these sorts of "*sub rosa* plan" objections gained some traction, especially in the Fifth Circuit.[10] But in most modern cases, so long as the sale process does not fully

---

[8]　*See* Bankruptcy Code § 365 and Chapter 5 of this book.

[9]　Stephanie Ben-Ishai & Stephen J. Lubben, *Involuntary Creditors and Corporate Bankruptcy*, 45 U. British Colum. L. Rev. 253 (2012).

[10]　In re Continental Air Lines, Inc., 780 F.2d 1223, 1228 (5th Cir. 1990); In re Braniff Airways, Inc., 700 F.2d 935, 939 (5th Cir. 1983).

dictate the terms of a future plan, the fact that a sale lacks the full protections of section 1129 is not itself a reason to stop the sale.[11]

The leading 363 decision, *Lionel*, overturned a bankruptcy court order approving the sale of a subsidiary because the debtor volunteered no "business justification" for avoiding the chapter 11 plan process.[12] Somewhat unpredictably, given that the sale was blocked in *Lionel*, that decision's "business justification" standard is used today to approve the vast bulk of 363 sales.[13] In particular, while in *Lionel* the debtor said it was proceeding by way of a sale to get a major creditor off its back, these days debtors proffer some plausible "business justification" for the sale, and the sale is normally approved.[14]

The major benefit provided by a bankruptcy court order approving an asset sale (or sale under a plan, but that is not our focus in this Chapter) is that the Debtors' assets are transferred to the purchaser free and clear of virtually all liens and claims. So long as the debtor gives its creditors notice of the sale, and thus provides sufficient due process as required by the Fifth Amendment, most state law successor liability doctrines can be avoided by conducting the sale in bankruptcy.[15] This contrasts with state corporate law that provides a structure for such sales, but does not protect the buyer to the same degree.

When the assets are sold free and clear of liens under section 363(f)(3), the cases are divided regarding whether the sale must exceed the face amount of the debt secured by the property to be

---

[11]   *See* In re Chrysler LLC, 576 F.3d 108, 119 (2d Cir. 2009) ("Consistent with an underlying purpose of the Bankruptcy Code—maximizing the value of the bankrupt estate—it was no abuse of discretion to determine that the Sale prevented further, unnecessary losses."), *judgment vacated as moot*, 592 F.3d 370 (2d Cir. 2010).

[12]   In re Lionel, 722 F.2d 1063, 1070-72 (2d Cir. 1983).

[13]   Melissa B. Jacoby & Edward J. Janger, *Ice Cube Bonds: Allocating the Price of Process in Chapter 11 Bankruptcy*, 123 YALE L.J. 862, 868 (2014) ("Under current practice, if the sale proponent offers a plausible business justification, the court can (and, we believe, usually does) approve it.").

[14]   In re Exaeris, Inc., 380 B.R. 741, 744 (Bankr. Del. 2008) ("The sale of assets which is not in the debtor's ordinary course of business requires proof that: (1) there is a sound business purpose for the sale; (2) the proposed sale price is fair; (3) the debtor has provided adequate and reasonable notice; and (4) the buyer has acted in good faith.")

[15]   In re Trans World Airlines, Inc., 322 F.3d 283 (3d Cir. 2003).

sold, or whether the sales price must exceed only the "value" of the secured claim as represented by the current value of the collateral. That is, does section 506 claim bifurcation apply in this context? Ideally the secured lender will consent to the sale – section 363(f)(2) – because sale through the bankruptcy auction process often obtains the best value for the assets, and if not the lender can take the assets through its credit bidding rights.

SUMMARY

363 are an important adjunct to the chapter 11 plan process. If the debtor's assets do not need serious restructuring, but instead the company simply needs to get out of from under excessive debt obligations, a quick sale can return the assets to productive use in a short period of time. The creditors can then argue about who should get what of the sale proceeds.

19. Prepacks

Key concepts:

- Exchange offers
- Pre-petition solicitation
- The limits of prepacks
- "Chapter 22"

As we have seen in the previous Chapters, chapter 11 can be a useful tool for addressing financial distress. But it is not without its costs, both direct (professional fees) and indirect (loss of business). Especially if it wants to avoid the latter sort of costs, a debtor might ideally negotiate a deal with its creditors outside of bankruptcy court.

But often the creditors are too scattered, or they cannot come to any consensus about what should be done with the debtor. If the debtor can get most, but not all, to agree to a deal, a quick trip into bankruptcy court can bind the rest.

This is the basic use of "prepackaged" chapter 11 cases. The debtor uses the formal bankruptcy process to bind holdout creditors to a workout deal that is backed by most creditors.

Out-of-court workouts or reorganization deals are often effectuated through an "exchange offer." This is a tender offer for the company's existing debt, in which new debt or equity is offered in place of the old. The goal is to either reduce existing debt loads, postpone maturity dates, or both.

When such exchange offers succeed, they often help the debtor-company avoid the need for any future bankruptcy filing. But the trick is that many exchange offers do not succeed.

Exchange offers are voluntary procedures: creditors decide for themselves whether they want to participate, and there is no ability to "cramdown" the offer on a dissenting few. Thus, the debtor needs to make the offer attractive enough for the bulk of creditors to accept it, while at the same time achieving the degree of debt relief needed to stave off a bankruptcy filing. Sometimes it is simply impossible to balance both of these conflicting goals.

Moreover, there is a good bit of logic in a creditor strategy of declining the exchange offer, yet hoping that it will succeed. In such a case, the creditor retains its original debt instrument, but now faces a debtor with an improved balance sheet, because everybody else participated. Of course, once every creditor starts thinking that way, the entire process collapses.

To overcome these limitations on exchange offers, debtors will sometimes combine their exchange offer with a solicitation of votes on a prepackaged bankruptcy plan. If the exchange offer fails, but there are enough votes in favor of the plan,[1] the same deal is implemented by a quick trip through chapter 11. And in some cases, the debtor will simply jump right to the solicitation on the bankruptcy plan, and skip the exchange offer altogether.

A prepackaged plan – or more simply, a "prepack" – is a chapter 11 case that is filed with voting already complete for some classes of a proposed plan.[2] The debtor files the case, and immediately asks the court to schedule a combined hearing on both its disclosure statement and confirmation of the plan. Typically such a hearing will be scheduled about a month after the petition date. If all works as planned, the debtor will be in and out of bankruptcy before most counterparties will even notice.

So if Bogartco decides to revamp its balance sheet by way of a prepack, it would negotiate a plan with key creditor constituencies. Once it has those creditors on board, it would solicit votes from the broader group of creditors in that class. Often the creditors who were involved in initial negotiations will sign a "lock up"

---

[1] Bankruptcy Code § 1126(c) ("A class of claims has accepted a plan if such plan has been accepted by creditors, other than any entity designated under subsection (e) of this section, that hold at least two-thirds in amount and more than one-half in number of the allowed claims of such class held by creditors, other than any entity designated under subsection (e) of this section, that have accepted or rejected such plan.").

[2] Under English law, the term "pre-pack" refers instead to administrations under the Enterprise Act 2002, where the sale of the debtor business is negotiated before the appointment of administrators. The sale then completes either immediately upon – or shortly following – the appointment. In short, an English law pre-pack is more like the 363 sales discussed in Chapter 18 of this book.

agreement, whereby they agree to vote in favor of the plan as negotiated. In the meantime, Bogartco's counsel will prepare for a chapter 11 filing that will be scheduled to occur at the end of voting on the plan.

One vital point to keep in mind is that since there is, as yet, no bankruptcy case underway, and no bankruptcy estate has been formed, the vote solicitation takes place under non-bankruptcy law. Thus, if Bogartco solicited votes on the plan from shareholders, it would be subject to proxy rules under the 1934 Securities and Exchange Act. Requests that shareholders exchange existing shares for any new instrument would be tender offers subject to the Williams Act.[3] And new equity securities given to creditors under a plan might be subject to the requirements of filing a registration statement, and providing a prospectus, under the 1933 Securities Act.

As a result, prepacks are often directed only at bondholders and senior lenders. Moreover, the plan is typically structured to take advantage of key exemptions to the Securities Act, so that securities issued under the plan will not require a registration statement.[4]

Trade creditors and employees typically "ride through" the case, as if it did not happen. Shareholders, who often lose their entire stake in the company, are not solicited prepetition, as that would involve a proxy statement, subject to SEC approval. Rather, their vote against the plan is presumed under section 1126(g) and the plan is then crammed down on the shareholders under section 1129(b).

In combined exchange offer and prepack solicitations, the exchange offer is conditioned on getting a sufficient number of bondholders to participate (often at least 85 percent) and, if that fails but the debtor has sufficient votes under section 1126 (two thirds in amount and half in number), the bankruptcy plan will implement the same basic deal as proposed by the exchange offer.

Because prepacks get the debtor in and out of bankruptcy so quickly, nearly every debtor, and every manager, who has heard of a prepack wants to do their bankruptcy that way. But a prepack is a

---

[3]   15 U.S.C. §§ 78m(d)–(e), 78n(d)–(f).

[4]   In particular, the exemptions under §§ 3(a)(9) and 4(a)(2) of the Securities Act of 1933. Solicitation might also be limited to institutional investors, those that qualify under Rule 144A, or offshore investors under Regulation S.

useful tool for conducting a balance sheet restructuring, and not every debtor's problems will be solved by simply repairing the balance sheet. Debtors that need to use the other tools in the Bankruptcy Code – avoidance actions, assumption and rejection of contracts, assets sales – are better served by filing a more traditional chapter 11 case.

In addition, it is undoubtedly true that many debtors that undergo a prepack find themselves back in chapter 11 just a year or two later. This "chapter 22" phenomena might suggest the overuse of prepacks by debtors that would be candidates for a more traditional chapter 11 process. This might be particularly true when we consider the cost of running two chapter 11 cases, in place of one.

SUMMARY

Prepacks are an attempt at achieving the "best of both worlds." The process touches the Bankruptcy Code ever so slightly, while binding holdouts to a deal to a greater extent than would be possible in a traditional out-of-court workout. But the speedy process is not for all debtors, and it is up to counsel (and financial advisers) to guide the client to the appropriate tool for a particular situation.

20. The effects of plan confirmation

Key concepts:

- Binding effect of plan
- Effective dates
- Chapter 11 discharge
- Non-dischargeable "claims"
- Third-party releases

Upon plan confirmation, either consensually under section 1129(a) or via cramdown and section 1129(b), the debtor begins to resume normal operations. Section 1141, our focus in this Chapter, sets forth the implications of a confirmed plan for the debtor and its stakeholders. As discussed in further detail below, many aspects of section 1141 are subject to being overridden by either the plan itself or the bankruptcy court's order confirming the plan – the "confirmation order." Thus, it is important to consider section 1141 together with both the plan and the confirmation order.

Section 1141(a) states that the provisions of a confirmed plan bind the debtor, and essentially anyone else connected to the debtor.[1] A confirmed chapter 11 plan binds a party regardless of whether that party voted to accept the plan or whether that party's claim or interest was impaired.

The plan and the confirmation order replace all pre-existing rights against the debtor. As a result, a creditor should not expect to collaterally attack a confirmation order; rather, in keeping with the collective nature of bankruptcy, all arguments must be raised as part of the bankruptcy, and the confirmation process in particular. Even

---

[1] Provided they have constitutionally adequate notice – indeed, many courts have held that chapter 11 cases require that parties must have notice of the claims bar date and the hearing on the confirmation of the proposed plan if the plan is to be binding on those parties.

provisions that are arguably inappropriate will bind parties who had proper notice, unless the confirmation order is timely appealed.

Sometimes the plan dictates that the effective date is the confirmation date. That usually only works if the court is willing to reduce the period for filing appeals.[2] In many cases, the effective date happens when certain specified conditions have been satisfied. In this respect, a chapter 11 plan is just like other corporate transactions, with a closing date somewhat after the date the deal is signed (or in this case, approved by the court). Typical closing conditions will include, somewhat obviously, entry of the confirmation order. Others include execution of the revised corporate documents (bylaws, certificate of incorporation, etc.) for the debtor and any relevant debt agreements for securities issued under the plan.

Under section 1141(b), except as otherwise provided in the plan or confirmation order, confirmation of the plan vests all of the property of the estate in the debtor as of the effective date of the plan. With this transfer, the automatic stay ends its reign over the debtor's property, but as we will see, the bankruptcy discharge, set forth in section 1141(d)(1), performs a similar function.

In particular, section 1141(d) "discharges the debtor from any debt that arose before the date of such confirmation." That is, the debtor no longer has any liability for pre-confirmation claims, save for the obligations set forth in the plan and confirmation order.[3]

In keeping with the rule that business debtors do not get a discharge in chapter 7 cases, section 1141(d) does contain an exception for cases where the debtor is liquidating. In short, the debtor is not discharged if it liquidates in chapter 11 and would have been denied a discharge in chapter 7.[4] Otherwise, the corporation receives a broad discharge, subject to only limited exceptions for certain taxes, "whistleblower" claims, and customs duties.

The scope of this discharge is much broader than the scope of the discharge granted in a chapter 7, which applies only to individuals

---

[2]   Bankruptcy Rule 3020(e).

[3]   Note that § 1141(d)(1) expressly states that its general rule can be modified by other provisions of subsection (d), in the confirmed plan, or in the order confirming that plan.

[4]   This can be avoided by keeping some small part of the debtor operating after confirmation, even if the bulk of the debtor liquidates.

and only to debts that arose before the order for relief was entered.[5] So, in a chapter 11 case, a debtor could be discharged from debts that arose after the petition date but before plan confirmation.

A chapter 11 discharge applies only to "claims" that "arose" before confirmation and are held by creditors who received constitutionally sufficient notice of the bankruptcy. The debtor's liability creates a claim only if it gives rise to a right to payment.[6] If a liability does not constitute a claim, it cannot be discharged, and the debtor will retain the liability after emerging from bankruptcy protection.

So, when assessing whether a discharge affects a specific liability, we need to consider if we are dealing with a "claim" under the Code, whether that claim "arose" before confirmation, and did the creditor holding the claim receive sufficient notice of the bankruptcy case, the chapter 11 plan, and the ability to participate meaningfully in the bankruptcy process. If the answer to all questions is "yes," then the claim is discharged unless excepted from discharge under section 1141.

In some cases, environmental cleanup obligations have been held not to be claims, and thus not dischargeable. Monetary claims for cleanup costs incurred prepetition and monetary claims for future response costs arising solely from prepetition releases of hazardous wastes are generally considered unsecured, dischargeable claims. But an injunction that prohibits ongoing pollution or that demands cleanup of property the debtor intends to retain post-bankruptcy may not be dischargeable through bankruptcy, inasmuch as the injunction does not represent a right to payment of money.

And as a result of non-bankruptcy law, a debtor might not fully escape its liability for unpaid retirement benefits. In particular, if a pension plan is terminated during a bankruptcy proceeding, then the termination claims are not claims in the terminating employers' bankruptcy cases, but instead become obligations of the employers

---

[5] Typically, the petition date, at least in voluntary cases.
[6] Bankruptcy Code § 101(5).

only upon their emergence from bankruptcy.[7] That means that these liabilities are essentially non-dischargeable in a chapter 11 reorganization.

A debtor facing substantial environmental or pension liabilities might consider selling its "good" assets in a 363 sale and then liquidating the remainder.[8] Environmental or pension regulators must watch to ensure that the sale proceeds are not paid out to creditors before their special claims are addressed.

Supporting the discharge in subpart (d) is section 1141(c), which provides that property dealt with by the plan is free and clear of all claims and interests of creditors, equity security holders and general partners of the debtor. Subsection (c) not only gives the debtor back its property, free of pre-bankruptcy liens, but also extinguishes claims and interests of equity holders or general partners of the debtor.

Section 1141(c) clearly states that "the property dealt with by the plan is free and clear of all claims and interests of creditors, equity holders, and of general partners in the debtors." That would seem to be the end of the story, but several Courts of Appeal have cited old Bankruptcy Act case law for the proposition that liens "ride through" the bankruptcy if the secured creditor does not participate in the case.[9]

Can a secured creditor "sit out" the chapter 11 process, and choose not to "participate" in a case to avoid application of a core aspect of chapter 11? That seems to be the implication of these Circuit Court opinions, but that does not make any sense. Nowhere in section 1141(c) is the binding effect of discharge on a creditor predicated upon a creditor's participation in the chapter 11 case, and we can only hope that the Supreme Court rectifies this sooner rather than later.

If the secured creditor does participate, most courts agree that a chapter 11 plan can be used to cut down the creditor's lien to the value of the collateral. That is, when the claim is bifurcated under

---

[7]   29 U.S.C. § 1306(a)(7)(B); *see also* Pension Benefit Guaranty Corporation v. Oneida Ltd., 562 F.3d 154 (2d Cir. 2009).

[8]   *See generally* Stephanie Ben-Ishai & Stephen J. Lubben, *Sales or Plans: A Comparative Account of the "New" Corporate Reorganization*, 56 McGILL L.J. 591 (2011). *See also* Chapter 18 of this book.

[9]   *E.g.*, In re Northern New Eng. Tel. Operations, LLC, 795 F.3d 343 (2d Cir. 2015).

section 506, the post-bankruptcy lien can be limited to the amount of the allowed secured claim.[10] This is in contrast to the rule in chapter 7, under the Supreme Court's (arguably erroneous) holding in *Dewsnup v. Timm*, which barred chapter 7 debtors from stripping a creditor's partially-secured claim down to the value of the collateral securing it.[11]

Although debtors obtain a discharge of their liabilities upon confirmation of a plan of reorganization, section 524(e) of the Bankruptcy Code provides that the discharge "does not affect the liability of any other entity on, or the property of any other entity for, such [pre-confirmation] debt."

Plans nonetheless sometimes provide for the release of third parties, including officers, directors, creditors' committees and their members, new investors, and often their professionals, advisers and the like. These releases are commonly referred to as "third-party releases." Whether such releases are permissible, and whether such releases can bind those who do not consent in their granting, is the subject of conflicting case law.[12]

If Bogartco's subsidiary – HatCo – is in chapter 11, Bogartco might contribute funds to the reorganization plan in exchange for a release of any claims that might be brought against it, as controlling shareholder of the debtor. In mass-tort cases, a release might be granted to an insurance company that contributes funds – up to the policy limit – to the debtor's plan.

Section 1142(a) expressly provides that the debtor shall implement the plan notwithstanding any otherwise applicable nonbankruptcy law or regulation relating to financial condition that may restrict the debtor from doing so. State laws conditioned on solvency or payment of discharged debts, for example, will not thwart the plan. Section 1142(b) then provides that the court may order parties to execute and deliver documents that are necessary to implement the plan. This helps prevent a disappointed creditor from exercising an effective veto over the implementation of the plan.

---

[10] Remember the creditor can avoid this fate by making the § 1111(b) election, as discussed in Chapter 15.

[11] Discussed in Chapter 4.

[12] Absent consent of the releasing party, such releases are generally prohibited in the Fifth, Ninth, and Tenth Circuits as well as the D.C. Circuit. Courts in the Second, Fourth, Sixth, Seventh and Eleventh Circuits permit consensual releases and, in some circumstances, have approved releases without consent.

When the case has been fully administered, Code section 350 provides for the case to be closed.

SUMMARY

Regardless of how the debtor achieves a confirmed plan, confirmation has several important implications. First, the debtor formally regains its property – the "estate" ceases to exist – and begins operations outside of the protection of the Code. Next, that property is returned to the debtor free of the claims and interests of its old creditors, except as preserved by the terms of the plan. And the debtor is protected from creditor action by the discharge, which is effectively a permanent form of the automatic stay.

21. Small businesses in chapter 11

> **Key concepts**:
>
> - Small Business Reorganization Act
> - SBRA trustees
> - Cramdown and disposable income

The old 1898 Bankruptcy Act, after amendment during the New Deal, featured separate chapters for publicly traded and smaller business debtors. Chapter X provided for a trustee and an active role for the SEC in the "big cases," while chapter XI was less formal, and eventually did not even require compliance with the absolute priority rule. As a result, many larger businesses tried to shoehorn their way into chapter XI, resulting in myriad legal disputes over the appropriateness of this move, and the drafters of the 1978 Bankruptcy Code thought that this was best avoided by having a single, unified business provision – modern chapter 11.

However, in doing so, small businesses were saddled with all of the elaborate provisions – like creditors committees – that really only made sense when applied to more substantial estates. Moreover, the 2005 amendments to the Code, known mostly for their deep skepticism toward personal bankruptcy relief, exhibited an analogous hostility toward small business debtors.[1] Firm time limits were imposed on such debtors with few resources offered to help the business work through chapter 11 on such an accelerated

---

[1] Robert M. Lawless, *Small Business and the 2005 Bankruptcy Law: Should Mom and Apple Pie Be Worried*, 31 S. ILL. U. L.J. 585 (2007) ("The 2005 bankruptcy law ... was affirmatively hostile to small business, making it more difficult for small businesses and their owners to get bankruptcy relief").

schedule.[2] In addition, the debtor-firm was burdened with additional disclosure obligations.[3] As Congress reported at the time, these provisions were "designed to weed out small business debtors who are not likely to reorganize."[4] Ultimately, the 2005 amendments simply discouraged small business use of chapter 11 altogether.

Some commentators argued that these unsympathetic provisions, combined with the general costs of using chapter 11, encouraged the use of non-bankruptcy reorganization mechanisms – like assignments for the benefit of creditors and receiverships. The American Bankruptcy Institute's Commission to Study the Reform of chapter 11 likewise found that the potential to lose control of a business, through strict application of the absolute priority rule in a cramdown and the need to come up with substantial new money to fund a "new value" plan,[5] also led most founders to avoid the Bankruptcy Code at all costs.[6]

Building from the ABI's findings, and with the support of the National Bankruptcy Conference, Congress revisited the question of small business bankruptcy anew in 2019. The result was the bipartisan Small Business Reorganization Act of 2019 (or the "SBRA"), which enacts a new subchapter V of chapter 11 for small business debtors.[7]

Subchapter V only applies to eligible debtors who elect to use the new subchapter. In particular, Bankruptcy Code section 101(51D) defines a small business debtor as a person:

---

[2] Bankruptcy Code §§ 308, 1121(e). Section 1121(e) remains a potential issue for those debtors who do not engage the new SBRA that is otherwise the subject of this Chapter.

[3] Bankruptcy Code §§ 308, 1116. In contrast to section 1121(e), both of these 2005 sections apply even if the small business debtor has elected to be covered by the SBRA; in particular, new section 1187 provides that section 308 and paragraphs (2) through (7) of section 1116 apply in such cases. As Professor Lawless has noted, in theory section 308 applies even outside of chapter 11, given its placement within chapter 3. Lawless, *supra* note 1, at 592–93. Interesting, the Bankruptcy Rules seem to assume that section 308 only applies in chapter 11. Rule 2015(a)(6). *Accord* Official Form 425C. Professor Lawless seems to have the better of the argument, since small business case is defined only to include chapter 11, while small business debtor, the term at issue in section 308, is not so limited. Compare Bankruptcy Code § 101(51C) and § 101(51D).

[4] H.R. Rep. No. 109-31, at 19 (2005).

[5] *See* Chapter 17.

[6] http://bit.ly/ABIsmallb.

[7] Pub. L. No. 116-54, 133 Stat. 1079.

engaged in commercial or business activities (including any affiliate ... and excluding a person whose primary activity is the business of owning single asset real estate) that has aggregate noncontingent liquidated secured and unsecured debts ... in an amount not more than $2,725,625 (excluding debts owed to 1 or more affiliates or insiders) not less than 50 percent of which arose from the commercial or business activities of the debtor.[8]

The definition further excludes publicly traded companies and companies that are part of corporate groups that either exceed the debt limits collectively or where any member of the group is publicly traded.[9]

The groups point is a bit tricky, because a close reading of section 101(51D)(B), which bars the groups, refers to "any member of a group of affiliated *debtors* that has aggregate noncontingent liquidated secured and unsecured debts in an amount greater than" the debt cap. Under 101(13), the "term 'debtor' means person or municipality concerning which a case under this title has been commenced." As a result, it appears that the cap only applies to members of a group that actually file for bankruptcy and thus just a part of a corporate group, with total debts less than the cap, might be able to file under the SBRA, so long as no entity in the entire group (filing and non-filing) is publicly traded.[10]

"Person" is a defined term in the Code, which picks up "individuals, partnerships, and corporation[s]."[11] In short, the new SBRA can be utilized by any business, regardless of form, including sole proprietorship, so long as more than half of the debts come from commercial or business activities. The benefit to such a debtor of electing into the SBRA is a process that tempers the normal chapter

---

[8] The CARES Act, passed by Congress to address the economic impact of the COVID-19 pandemic, temporarily increased the debt limit to $7,500,000 for one year. After one year, running to March 2021, the debt limit was to return to $2,725,625. In March 2021, Congress extended the increased limit for a further year. It would not be surprising if Congress eventually make this increase permanent. Also note that the dollar figure here – presumably whatever number is eventually settled on – is subject to periodic adjustment, like most other dollar figures in the Code. *See supra* page 32, note 34.

[9] Publicly traded is defined as being subject to reporting requirements under the Exchange Act.

[10] Bankruptcy Code § 101(51D)(B)(ii) keeps out the publicly traded companies themselves, and subparagraph (iii) keeps out affiliates of publicly traded companies.

[11] Bankruptcy Code § 101(41).

11 requirements, especially with regard to plan confirmation, with concepts imported from chapter 12 (farm bankruptcy) and chapter 13 (personal reorganization).

Because the definition of "small business debtor" also includes "affiliates" of the debtor, in theory the owner or shareholder of a debtor might also file along with the entity debtor as well, just so long as the total "noncontingent liquidated secured and unsecured debts as of the date of the filing of the petition" do not exceed the cap. This is not limited to business debts, so a (formerly) wealthy owner might well have personal obligations – credit cards, car loans and mortgages – that would push the combined debtor group over the cap. In that case, the entity can still file under SBRA, but the owner would have to seek separate personal bankruptcy relief.

Yet the key thing is that the debtor has to elect into subchapter V. Indeed, the Code strangely defines a small business *case* to be a case "in which the debtor is a small business debtor and has *not* elected that subchapter V of chapter 11 of this title shall apply."[12] That is, as a formal matter under the Code, a subchapter V case is *not* a small business case, despite what normal speakers of English might honestly believe. Instead, a SBRA case involves a small business *debtor*, while not being a small business *case*.

Once triggered, the SBRA declares about two dozen sections and subsections of chapter 11 to be inapplicable in subchapter V cases, a half-dozen of which may become re-applicable if the court so orders "for cause."[13] Unlike traditional chapter 11, a trustee will be appointed to each small-business debtor case. The SBRA's sponsors explain that the trustee will "perform duties similar to those performed by a ... Chapter 13 trustee and help ensure the reorganization stays on track." That is, the debtor – or more precisely, the debtor's management – stays in control, but the trustee is there to provide some oversight.[14]

---

[12] Bankruptcy Code § 101(51D) (emphasis added). Section 362(n) makes the automatic stay inapplicable in certain circumstances when the debtor in the current case is or was a debtor in a pending or previous small business case. Because a subchapter V debtor is not in a small business case, section 362(n) will not apply in a later case of the subchapter V debtor, which allows for multiple filings under the SBRA if the first plan proves overly optimistic.

[13] Bankruptcy Code § 1181(a).

[14] And in non-consensual plans the trustee acts a payment agent under the plan.

Specifically, section 1183(b)(7) states that "The trustee shall ... facilitate the development of a consensual plan of reorganization." Both the stated preference for a consensual plan and the suggestion that a trustee might help the debtor achieve such a plan are unique to the SBRA. Essentially the trustee might well function as a kind of "at the ready" mediator in plan negotiations.

While there is a trustee, there is no committee. SBRA amends section 1102(a)(3) to provide that no committee of unsecured creditors is appointed in any case of a small business debtor unless the court orders otherwise.[15]

Only a debtor may file a chapter 11 plan in a case under subchapter V.[16] Many commentators have written that the SBRA does away with the chapter 11 disclosure statement. It would be more accurate to say that a disclosure statement is still required, but the disclosure statement in subchapter V will be a "lite version" as compared with the traditional chapter 11 statement, and there is no general requirement that the disclosure statement contain "adequate information," as is the normal chapter 11 requirement.[17]

Indeed, only three items are required to be disclosed: a brief history of the business operations of the debtor, a liquidation analysis and projections of the ability of the debtor to make payments under the proposed plan. It is plainly contemplated that the plan and the statement will be a single document.[18] Nevertheless, both the liquidation analysis and the projections of future operations may still require small business debtors to achieve a new, higher level of financial sophistication, even if the SBRA disclosure statement requirements at least meet these debtors halfway.

The debtor has the choice of two tracks to get a plan confirmed, both set forth in section 1191. A consensual plan under 1191 needs to meet all, save one, of the requirements of section 1129(a).[19] The SBRA encourages consensual confirmation, and at an early status

---

[15] This applies whether or not the debtor has elected to proceed under subchapter V.

[16] Bankruptcy Code § 1189(a).

[17] *See* Chapter 15.

[18] Bankruptcy Code § 1190(1).

[19] Bankruptcy Code § 1191(a). The requirement that is excluded is paragraph (a)(15), which allows any single creditor to require an individual chapter 11 debtor to apply all of her disposable income toward making payments under the plan. As

conference in the case the debtor must file, and serve on the trustee and all parties in interest, a report that "details the efforts the debtor has undertaken and will undertake to attain a consensual plan of reorganization."[20]

However, if the debtor cannot achieve a consensual plan, section 1191(b) allows for a special type of cramdown. In what the SBRA terms an "exception" to 1191(a) consensual confirmation, section 1191(b) provides that

> if all of the applicable requirements of section 1129(a) of this title, other than paragraphs (8), (10), and (15) of that section, are met with respect to a plan, the court, on request of the debtor, shall confirm the plan notwithstanding the requirements of such paragraphs if the plan does not discriminate unfairly, and is fair and equitable, with respect to each class of claims or interests that is impaired under, and has not accepted, the plan.

So cramdown is possible under the SBRA even if no class has approved the plan – that's section 1129(a)(10), which is excluded in the SBRA – permitting the debtor to put forward a simple plan without the need to engage in any sort of contortions to find a group of friendly creditors who will play along.

If you have already read Chapter 17 of this book, you will also recognize that the concepts of "unfair discrimination" and "fair and equitable" have a long history in chapter 11 and its predecessor statutes. Yet although section 1191 uses the same terminology, it gives the terms new definitions.

With regard to secured creditors, it turns out that very little has changed, since 1191(c)(1) refers us right back to 1129(b). That means that dissenting secured creditors will get the present value of their claim, and have the continued option of making a 1111(b) election.[21]

---

we will see, *infra*, SBRA has a different, creditor class-based, disposable income requirement. For the general requirements of 1129(a), *see* Chapter 16.

[20]   Bankruptcy Code § 1188(c).

[21]   *See* Chapter 17. If the debtor is an individual – a sole proprietorship – the debtor can sometimes cut her home loan down to the value of the collateral, something that is typically not possible in a routine personal bankruptcy case. The new rule in section 1190(3) authorizes modification of mortgage lien rights when the "new value" that a debtor received for such lien was (1) "not used primarily to

With regard to unsecured creditors, however, section 1191(c) offers up something quite different, and indeed here there are no references to 1129(b) whatsoever. As an initial matter, that means that the so-called "absolute priority rule" is not part of the analysis, opening up the possibility that the founders of a small business will be able to retain their equity without worrying about whether their jurisdiction still follows the new value exception and how much "new value" they have to offer up to meet that exception.

Instead, the court simply has to find that the debtor is paying the most it reasonably can under the plan. More precisely, section 1191(c) requires the debtor to pay all of its projected disposable income – or value equal to that disposable income – over the course of three to five years.[22] Disposable income includes net income after "the payment of expenditures necessary for the continuation, preservation, or operation of the business of the debtor."[23] In essence, disposable income here substitutes for the absolute priority rule.

Notably, such a cramdown plan must also contain

appropriate remedies, which may include the liquidation of nonexempt assets, to protect the holders of claims or interests in the event that the payments are not made.[24]

Presumably a provision setting forth what constitutes a default under the plan, with automatic lifting of the stay if left unremedied by a certain time, would meet this requirement.

In addition to avoiding the absolute priority rule, cramdown confirmation under the SBRA opens up the possibility of paying

---

acquire" the residence and (2) instead was "used primarily" in the debtor's small business. *See* In re Ventura, 615 B.R. 1, 17 (Bankr. E.D.N.Y. 2020).

[22] The concept comes from chapter 12, where farmers must pay disposable income to keep their farms. A similar concept existed before 2005 in chapter 13, but after the 2005 amendments, disposable income in that chapter became partially linked to the infamous "means test" which is designed to keep certain debtors out of personal chapter 7 cases.

[23] Bankruptcy Code § 1191(d)(2). The subtle distinction between the two forms of payment in section 1191(c)(2) leaves open the possibility that the debtor could back load the payments, so long as the value distributed throughout the life of the plan equals the projected disposable income.

[24] Bankruptcy Code § 1191(c)(3)(B).

administrative claims over the life of the plan.[25] Presumably this could also enable a debtor to stretch out its "cure" payments on prepetition defaults when it assumes an executory contract.[26] And maybe even the debtor's counsel might see their fees paid over time, which opens up some interesting potential conflicts between the debtor and counsel as the plan is being drafted.

If the court confirms a cramdown plan, section 1141(d) does not apply, and confirmation does not result in a discharge. Instead, new section 1192 provides for a discharge until the plan is complete – similar to what happens in chapters 12 and 13.[27] If the plan is consensual, the debtor is discharged upon confirmation, as in traditional chapter 11 cases.

The timeline remains aggressive, but perhaps more achievable given the other changes made by the SBRA.[28]

Within 60 days after the filing, the court is required to hold a status conference "to further the expeditious and economical resolution" of the case.[29] As noted, at least 14 days before the status conference, the debtor must file a report detailing the efforts it has taken and will take to attain a consensual plan of reorganization – which presumably means that the debtor must make such efforts within the first 45 days of the case, if not sooner. The debtor must file a reorganization plan within 90 days after the petition date, unless the need for the extension is caused by circumstances "for which the debtor should not justly be held accountable."[30]

---

[25]   Bankruptcy Code § 1191(e). In a traditional chapter 11 case, administrative claims have to be paid in full at the time of the effective date (as defined in the plan – often when payments begin). Bankruptcy Code § 1129(a)(9).

[26]   *See* Chapter 5.

[27]   Yet without incorporating the hardship-discharge provisions of section 1328(b).

[28]   *See* In re Trepetin, 617 B.R. 841, 845–47 (Bankr. D. Md. 2020) ("The Court acknowledges that Congress contemplated an accelerated process for subchapter V cases, likely as a means to facilitate quicker and cheaper reorganizations. Congress also expressed, however, significant concern for small business debtors, wanting to provide them with a realistic option for reorganizing and saving their business operations").

[29]   Bankruptcy Code § 1188(a).

[30]   Bankruptcy Code § 1189(b). Note that while under the 2005 small business provisions the debtor had to get the plan confirmed in 90 days, under SBRA the debtor just needs to formulate the plan within 90 days.

SUMMARY

Chapter 11 was never particularly friendly to small businesses, and after 2005 many saw it as affirmatively hostile. The SBRA is designed to open up bankruptcy and chapter 11 as a real option for small businesses once again. Whether the federal courts will win back these sorts of cases in large amounts, especially in states where state law alternatives like receivership have been greatly improved in recent years, remains to be seen.[31]

---

[31] On the state law alternatives, see STEPHEN J. LUBBEN, THE LAW OF FAILURE: A TOUR THROUGH THE WILDS OF AMERICAN INSOLVENCY LAW (Cambridge U. Press 2018).

PART V

Transnational business bankruptcy under
chapter 15

22. An introduction to chapter 15 of the Bankruptcy Code

> **Key concepts:**
>
> - Foreign representatives
> - Main and non-main proceedings
> - Transnational corporate groups

For those who conceive of corporate bankruptcy as a purely domestic consideration, this book ends at Chapter 21. But these days even small businesses are apt to have some degree of foreign operations, if only in the form of a small Canadian outpost to the business, or a manufacturing plant in Mexico.

This Chapter provides an overview of chapter 15, designed to facilitate the "recognition" of foreign bankruptcy cases. It also briefly discusses the broader issues that arise in restructuring a transnational business.

Chapter 15 provides for the commencement of a bankruptcy case in this country that is ancillary or complementary to an insolvency proceeding pending in some other country. The chapter 15 case will support the foreign case and will not be a "full" bankruptcy case like a chapter 7 liquidation or a chapter 11 reorganization. The chapter is based on the Model Law on Cross-Border Insolvency prepared by the United Nations Commission on International Trade Law (UNCITRAL).[1]

---

[1] Section 1501(a) of the Bankruptcy Code sets forth the purpose and the following five objectives of chapter 15: (i) to encourage cooperation between courts of the United States (including the U.S. Trustee and appointed fiduciaries) and foreign courts in cross-border insolvency cases; (ii) to provide greater legal certainty for trade and investment; (iii) to promote the fair and efficient administration of cross-border insolvencies in a way that protects the interests of all creditors, the debtor and other interested entities; (iv) to protect and maximize the

Upon the filing of a petition for recognition – by a foreign representative, and after notice and a hearing – a foreign proceeding is given automatic and mandatory recognition in the United States under section 1517. A debtor cannot commence a chapter 15 case for itself, rather a case is only commenced by a foreign representative. Thus, the petitioner is typically a trustee or other official, sometimes even an officer of the debtor, appointed by the foreign court to act as "foreign representative."

The Bankruptcy Code requires that certain documents accompany the petition for recognition, such as a certified copy of the decision commencing the foreign proceeding and appointing the foreign representative; a certificate from the foreign court affirming the existence of such foreign proceeding and the appointment of the foreign representative; or any other acceptable evidence proving the existence of the proceeding and appointment. The petition for recognition should also be accompanied by a statement identifying all known foreign proceedings related to the debtor. All documents must be translated into English, if necessary.

After notice and hearing, section 1517 provides that the bankruptcy court must enter an order recognizing the foreign proceeding if the proceeding is a foreign main proceeding or a foreign non-main proceeding within the meaning of section 1502.[2] A foreign main proceeding is one pending in the country where the debtor has the center of its main interests (or "COMI"), while a foreign non-main proceeding is one pending in a foreign country where the debtor has an "establishment."[3]

In the absence of evidence to the contrary, the debtor's registered office is presumed to be the center of the debtor's main interests.[4] Case law in Europe establishes that this presumption can be rebutted by showing that the "head office" functions are carried out in a jurisdiction other than where the registered office is located,[5]

---

value of the debtor's assets; and (v) to facilitate the rescue of financially troubled businesses with the goal of protecting investments and preserving employment.

[2] The petition must also meet the § 1515 procedural requirements.

[3] Section 1502 defines "establishment" as "any place of operations where the debtor carries out a nontransitory economic activity."

[4] Bankruptcy Code § 1516(c).

[5] Bankruptcy Code § 1508.

and leading American decisions have rejected a mechanical application of the COMI rules.[6] But an insolvency proceeding filed in the chancery division of the High Court of Justice in England by an English corporation will be recognized as a foreign main proceeding.

On the other hand, an insolvency proceeding from the same court, filed by a French corporation that has substantial operations in the United Kingdom, would be recognized as a foreign non-main proceeding. The debtor's COMI is not in the U.K., but it "carries out a nontransitory economic activity" in the jurisdiction, and thus has an "establishment" there.

Unlike voluntary chapter 7 or 11 cases, and more like an involuntary case, the automatic stay does not go into effect when a chapter 15 petition is filed. Automatic relief is only granted upon recognition of a foreign *main* proceeding.[7] Certain discretionary relief under 1521 may be granted in a foreign proceeding as either main or non-main. Sometimes this discretionary relief can be used to make a non-main proceeding almost like a main proceeding in practical effect.

Chapter 15 is used in two typical scenarios. The first use, probably the ones the drafters of chapter 15 primarily envisioned, is by a foreign debtor that seeks to extend the effects of its bankruptcy proceeding to the United States. For example, a South Korean shipping company might file for bankruptcy in Seoul, but have the Korean bankruptcy case "recognized" in the United States and thus protect the company's American assets from creditors.

The other common use of chapter 15 is in conjunction with "schemes of arrangement" filed in England or other Commonwealth jurisdictions.[8] These schemes can be used to restructure a

---

[6]   In re Fairfield Sentry Ltd., 714 F.3d 127, 137-38 (2d Cir. 2013); In re Avanti Commc'ns Grp. PLC, 582 B.R. 603, 611 (Bankr. S.D.N.Y. 2018).

[7]   Section 1520(a)(1) states that upon recognition of a foreign proceeding, § 362 shall "apply with respect to the debtor and the property of the debtor that is within the territorial jurisdiction of the United States." This is narrower than in a traditional chapter 7 or 11 case, where the stay protects the estate as well as the debtor, and potentially operates worldwide.

[8]   Other jurisdictions (*e.g.*, Spain, Singapore, and the Netherlands) have recently adopted similar corporate law provisions. And the UK has adopted a new reorganization procedure that melds aspects of chapter 11 with the scheme process. *See* Oscar Couwenberg & Stephen J. Lubben, *Good Old Chapter 11 In A Pre-Insolvency World: The Growth Of Global Reorganization Options*, 46 N.C. J. Int'l L. 353 (2021).

company's debt, but are thought of as part corporate law (and not insolvency law) in the British tradition.[9] Nonetheless, they are routinely recognized under chapter 15 by American bankruptcy courts.

Schemes can be used by debtors that have only the faintest of connections to the jurisdiction hosting the scheme. For example, a Ukrainian company might have issued debt with an English choice of law clause. That company might restructure the debt under a scheme of arrangement filed in London, despite having all of its business operations outside the U.K. That scheme could in turn be recognized in the United States under chapter 15.[10] Between the U.S. and the U.K., the scheme will become binding on most institutional creditors, as they are likely to have sufficient contacts with at least one of London or New York, thus enabling the respective courts to enforce the scheme.

Chapter 15, and its counterparts as enacted throughout the world, addresses one aspect of modern business and financial distress. That is, when a firm has operations abroad, it can extend its bankruptcy process out from the home country, into other key jurisdictions, through the use of the chapter 15 recognition process.

But many large corporations operate in foreign jurisdictions through subsidiaries. That is, while the entire corporate group might be known worldwide as "Bogartco," often the corporate structure is actually comprised of dozens, if not hundreds, of distinct legal entities.

Chapter 15 does not solve this problem, except in the general way that Bogartco can file for chapter 11 in San Francisco, and its London subsidiary can seek to have its English "administration" recognized in the United States under chapter 15 too. But chapter 15 itself does not allow the San Francisco and London operations to be reorganized under a single plan, even though the corporate group operated as a single whole before bankruptcy.

One option might be to file chapter 11 cases in California for both entities, and then seek to get the chapter 11 recognized in the U.K. as a foreign main proceeding. This would require rebutting

---

[9] These are sometimes referred to as "pre-insolvency" proceedings, since insolvency would necessitate formal bankruptcy or insolvency procedures in many jurisdictions.

[10] Presumably as a non-main proceeding, finding some "establishment" in the U.K., based on the debt and other economic activity in the UK.

the presumption that the place of incorporation is the location of the COMI, but it might be done if all key business decisions were made in San Francisco. If most of the creditors are financial institutions with ties to the United States, another option might be to simply file two chapter 11 cases and hope for the best abroad.[11] Yet another permutation would be to file only the American holding company under chapter 11, and request court approval to transfer funds to the foreign subsidiary as if no bankruptcy had happened.

Nearly every jurisdiction – other than the United States and Canada – has some sort of trading while insolvent law, that requires directors of insolvent businesses to commence proceedings upon learning of the insolvency. In some jurisdictions these laws are enforced by provisions providing for personal liability of directors who fail to make such a filing. And some places even impose criminal liability for knowing failures to file an insolvency case.

Commencement of insolvency proceedings could easily and swiftly disrupt any plan to localize a debtor's restructuring in the United States. One way around this is to simply coordinate proceedings among the courts. There are many examples of this happening between U.S. and Canadian courts. There are also a few examples involving the U.S. and the U.K. After that, examples of successful coordination become harder to find. But hopefully the general "spirit" of chapter 15 and the UNCITRAL model law might encourage more consideration of such coordination in the future.

SUMMARY

With the globalization of finance and commercial activity has come increased recognition of the need for coordinated and parallel business bankruptcy regimes. Problems arise in national bankruptcy and insolvency systems with a geographical reach that does not match the reach of the economic activity that they address. Chapter 15 represents an improvement over past approaches, but as noted at the end of the chapter, the problem of corporate groups are still addressed with less than ideal tools.

---

[11] *See generally* Oscar Couwenberg & Stephen J. Lubben, *Corporate Bankruptcy Tourists*, 70 BUS. LAW. 719 (2015).

Index